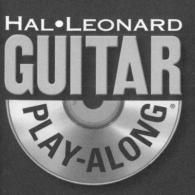

GUITAR PLAY-ALONG

PROGRESSIVE ROCK

ISBN 978-1-4234-9076-0

HAL•LEONARD®
CORPORATION

7777 W. BLUEMOUND RD. P.O. BOX 13819 MILWAUKEE, WI 53213

Visit Hal Leonard Online at
www.halleonard.com

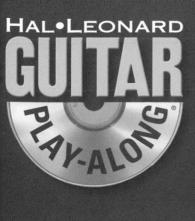

CONTENTS

Guitar Notation Legend

THE MUSICAL STAFF shows pitches and rhythms and is divided by bar lines into measures. Pitches are named after the first seven letters of the alphabet.

TABLATURE graphically represents the guitar fingerboard. Each horizontal line represents a string, and each number represents a fret.

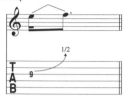
4th string, 2nd fret

1st & 2nd strings open, played together

open D chord

HALF-STEP BEND: Strike the note and bend up 1/2 step.

WHOLE-STEP BEND: Strike the note and bend up one step.

GRACE NOTE BEND: Strike the note and immediately bend up as indicated.

SLIGHT (MICROTONE) BEND: Strike the note and bend up 1/4 step.

BEND AND RELEASE: Strike the note and bend up as indicated, then release back to the original note. Only the first note is struck.

PRE-BEND: Bend the note as indicated, then strike it.

VIBRATO: The string is vibrated by rapidly bending and releasing the note with the fretting hand.

PALM MUTING: The note is partially muted by the pick hand lightly touching the string(s) just before the bridge.

HAMMER-ON: Strike the first (lower) note with one finger, then sound the higher note (on the same string) with another finger by fretting it without picking.

PULL-OFF: Place both fingers on the notes to be sounded. Strike the first note and without picking, pull the finger off to sound the second (lower) note.

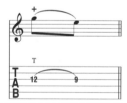

LEGATO SLIDE: Strike the first note and then slide the same fret-hand finger up or down to the second note. The second note is not struck.

SHIFT SLIDE: Same as legato slide, except the second note is struck.

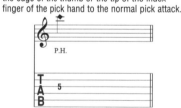

TRILL: Very rapidly alternate between the notes indicated by continuously hammering on and pulling off.

TAPPING: Hammer ("tap") the fret indicated with the pick-hand index or middle finger and pull off to the note fretted by the fret hand.

NATURAL HARMONIC: Strike the note while the fret-hand lightly touches the string directly over the fret indicated.

PINCH HARMONIC: The note is fretted normally and a harmonic is produced by adding the edge of the thumb or the tip of the index finger of the pick hand to the normal pick attack.

TREMOLO PICKING: The note is picked as rapidly and continuously as possible.

VIBRATO BAR DIVE AND RETURN: The pitch of the note or chord is dropped a specified number of steps (in rhythm), then returned to the original pitch.

VIBRATO BAR SCOOP: Depress the bar just before striking the note, then quickly release the bar.

VIBRATO BAR DIP: Strike the note and then immediately drop a specified number of steps, then release back to the original pitch.

Additional Musical Definitions

(accent) • Accentuate note (play it louder).

(staccato) • Play the note short.

D.S. al Coda • Go back to the sign (𝄋), then play until the measure marked *"To Coda,"* then skip to the section labelled **"Coda."**

D.C. al Fine • Go back to the beginning of the song and play until the measure marked *"Fine"* (end).

Fill

N.C.

• Label used to identify a brief melodic figure which is to be inserted into the arrangement.

• Harmony is implied.

• Repeat measures between signs.

• When a repeated section has different endings, play the first ending only the first time and the second ending only the second time.

Breathe

Words by Roger Waters
Music by Roger Waters, David Gilmour and Rick Wright

Intro

Slowly ♩ = 65

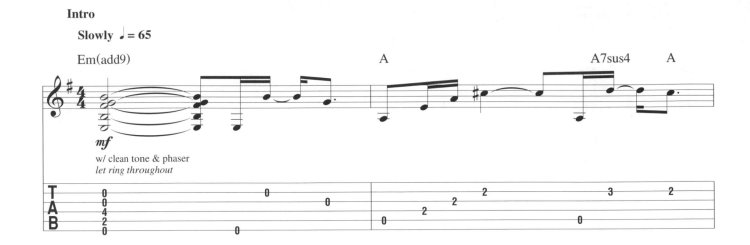

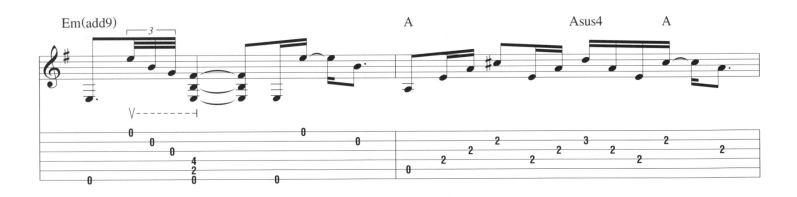

Verse

1. Breathe, _____ breathe in the air. _____

Don't be a - fraid __ to care. _____

Leave, __ but don't __ leave me. __

Look a - round, _____ (and) choose your own __ ground. (For)

8

long you live __ and high you fly, (and) smiles you'll give __ and tears you'll cry. And

all you touch __ and all __ you see is all your life __ will ev - er be.

Verse

2. Run, __ rab - bit, run. __

Dig that hole, _____ for - get __ the sun. _____

Tom Sawyer

Words by Neil Peart and Pye Dubois
Music by Geddy Lee and Alex Lifeson

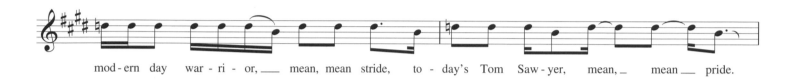

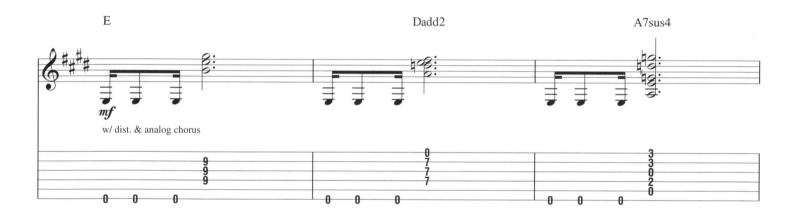

Chorus

The world is, the world __ is. Love and life are deep, __

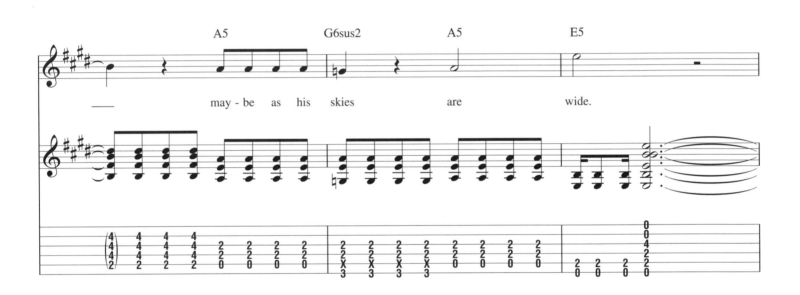

__ may - be as his skies are wide.

To - day's Tom Saw - yer, he gets high on you, __ and the

Interlude

N.C.(E)

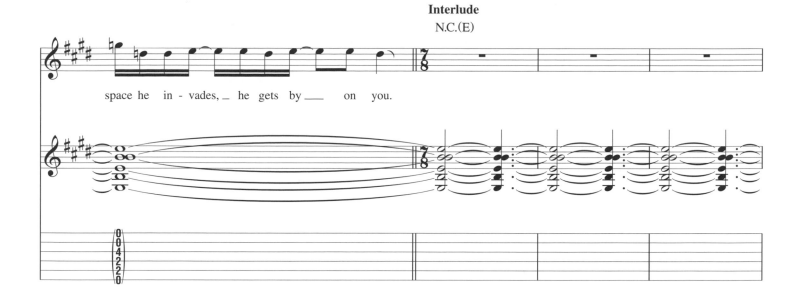

space he in - vades, _ he gets by ___ on you.

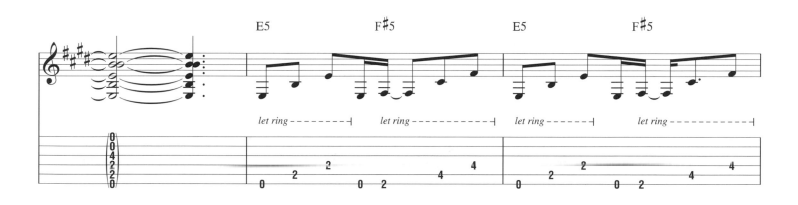

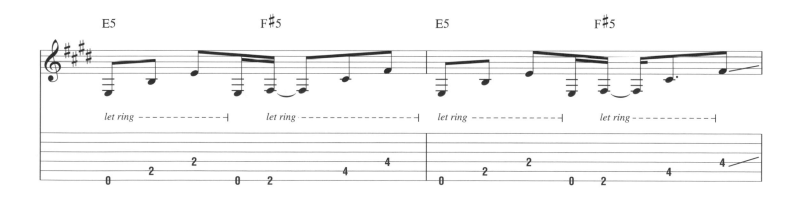

N.C.(E)

Guitar Solo

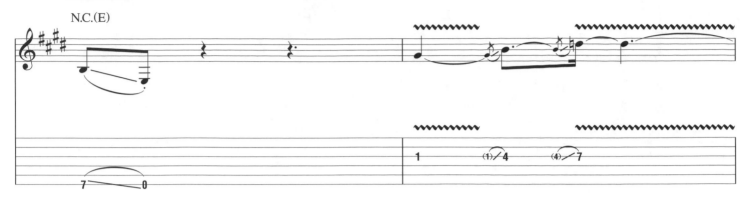

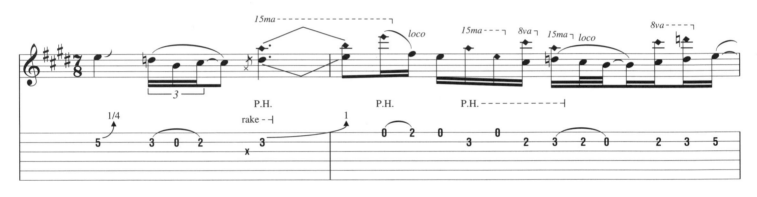

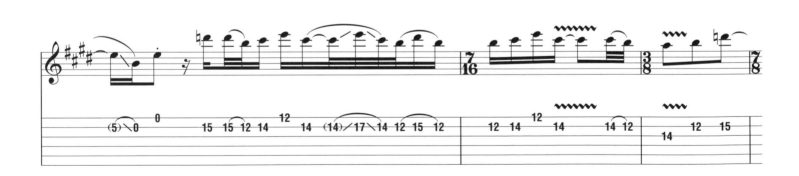

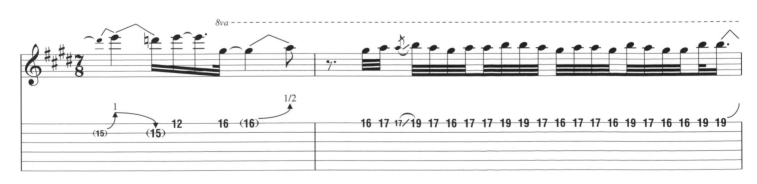

16

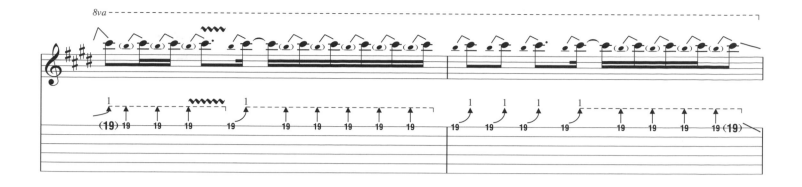

Interlude

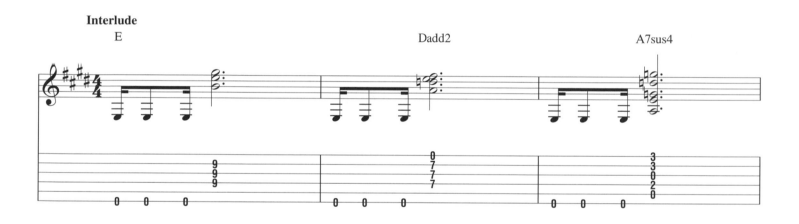

Verse

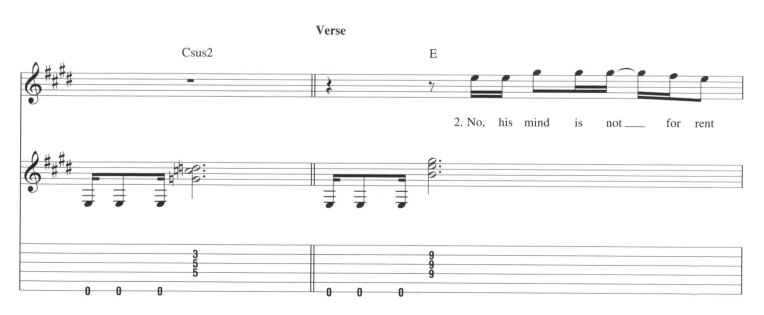

2. No, his mind is not___ for rent

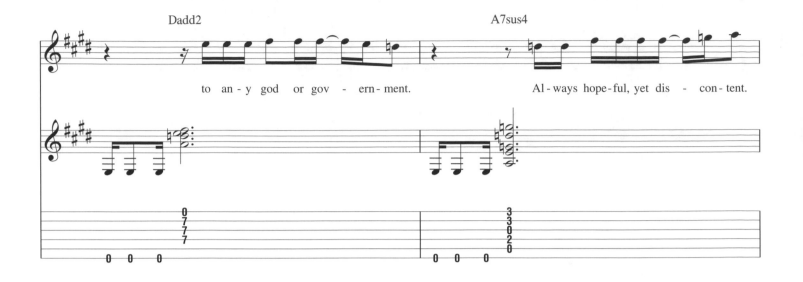

to an - y god or gov - ern - ment.   Al - ways hope - ful, yet dis - con - tent.

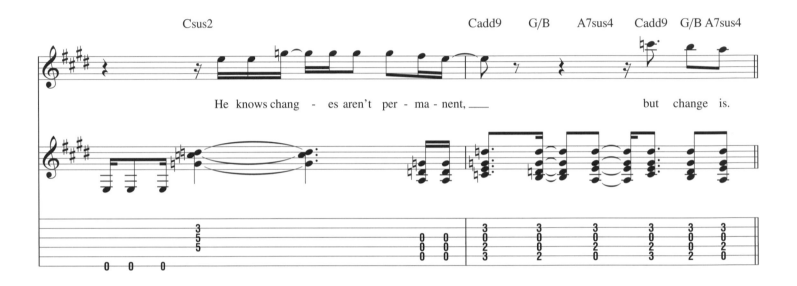

He knows chang - es aren't per - ma - nent, ___   but change is.

Interlude

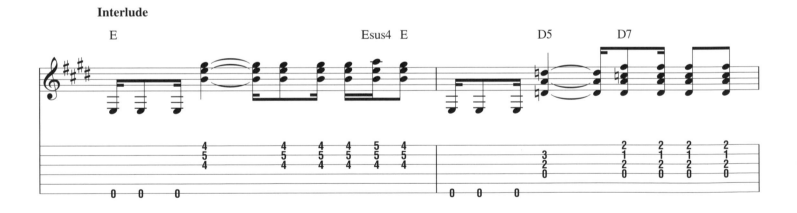

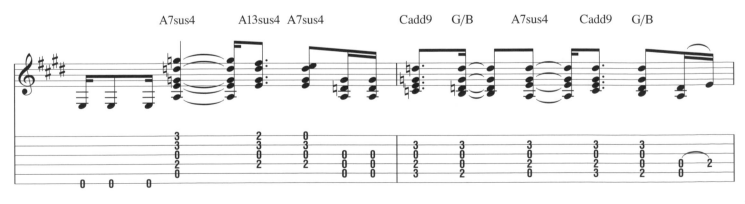

Chorus

The world is, the world __ is. Love and life are deep, __

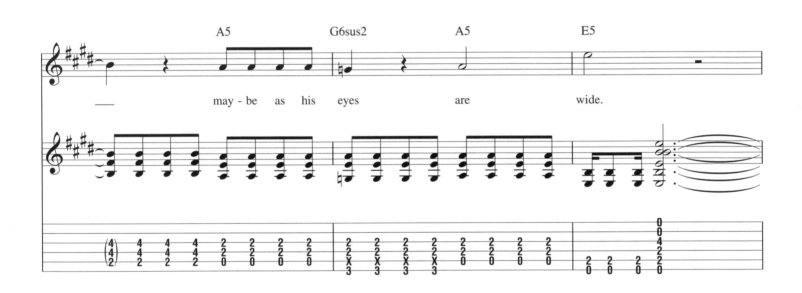

__ may - be as his eyes are wide.

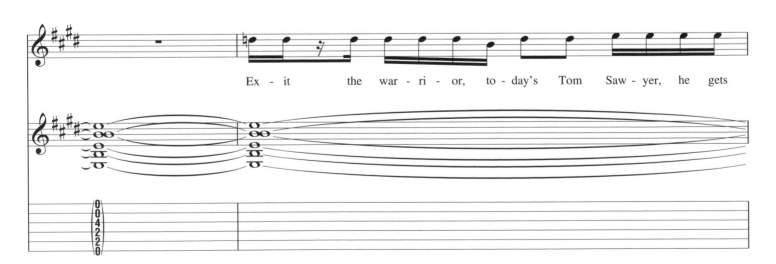

Ex - it the war - ri - or, to - day's Tom Saw - yer, he gets

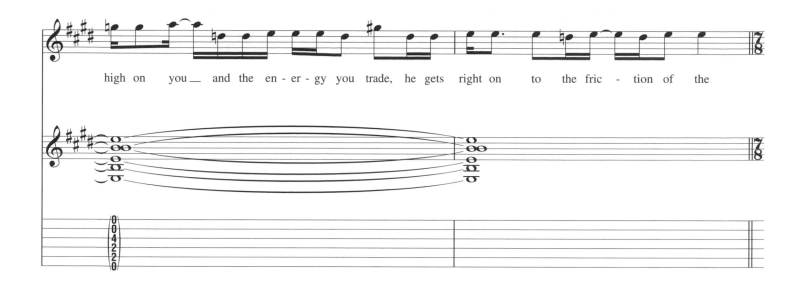

high on you___ and the en - er - gy you trade, he gets right on   to   the fric - tion of the

Outro

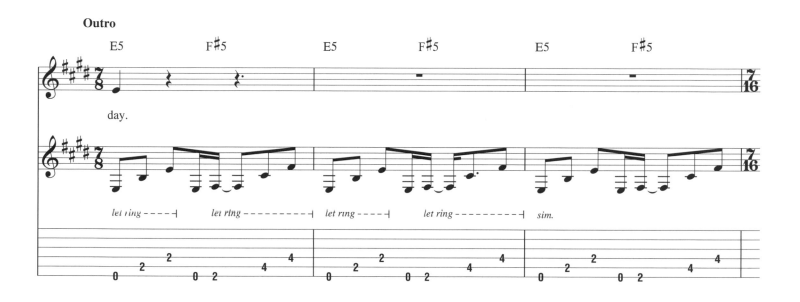

day.

let ring — — — — ⌐   let ring — — — — — — — — ⌐   let ring — — — — ⌐   let ring — — — — — — — — ⌐   sim.

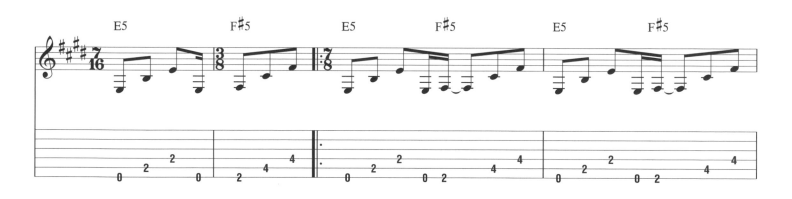

Repeat and fade

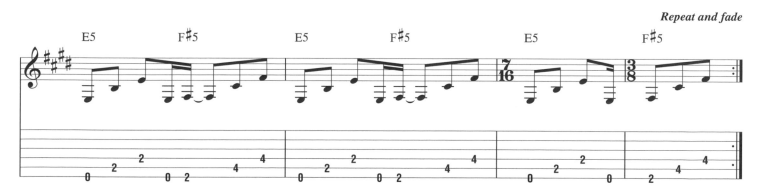

From the Beginning

Words and Music by Greg Lake

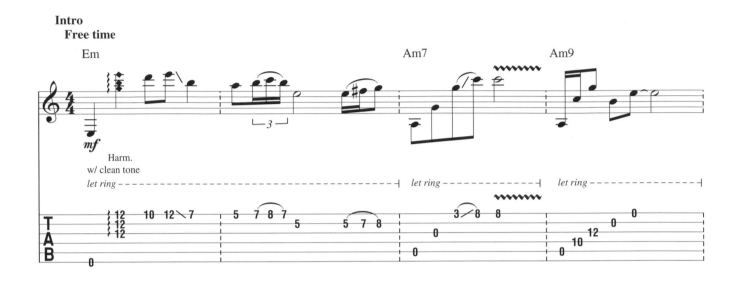

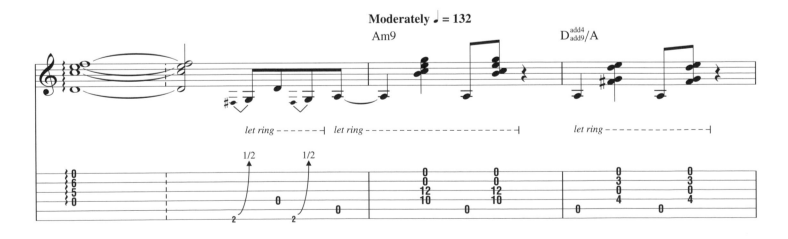

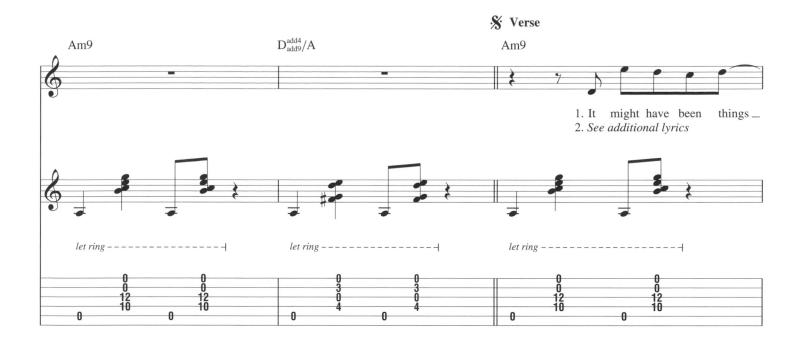

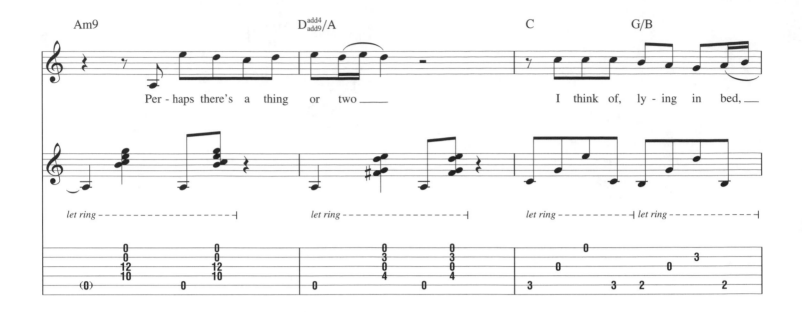

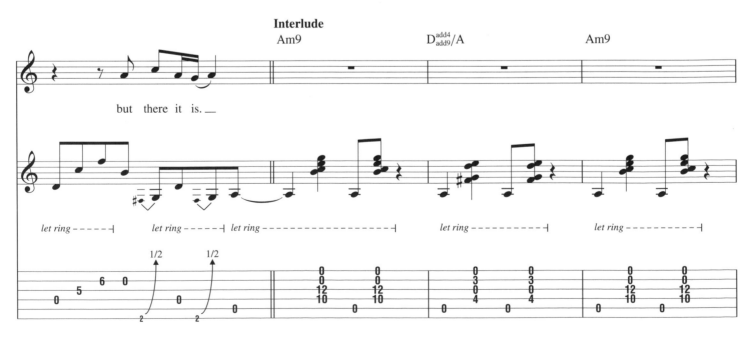

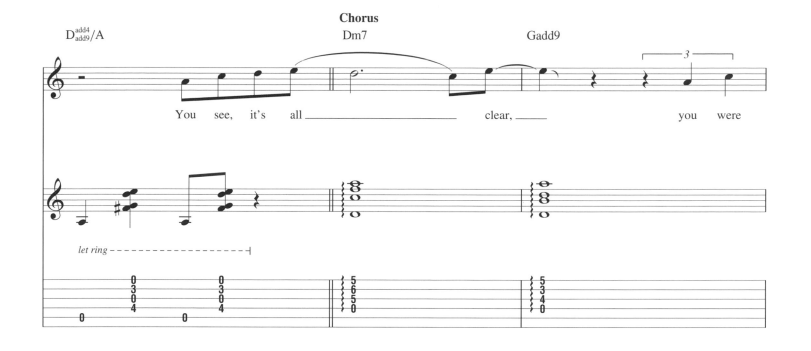

Chorus

D$_{add9}^{add4}$/A   Dm7   Gadd9

You see, it's all _____ clear, _____ you were

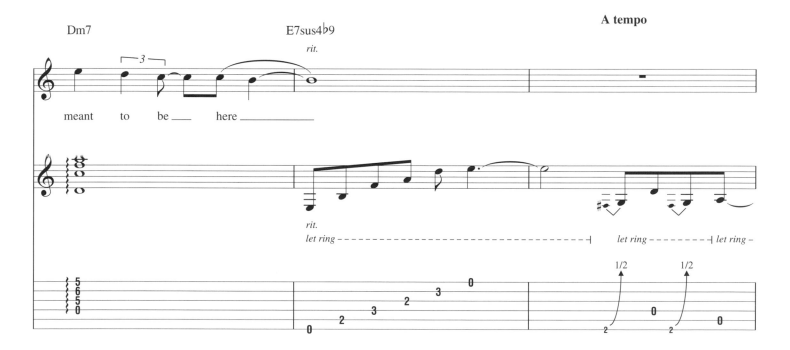

Dm7   E7sus4♭9   *rit.*   **A tempo**

meant to be __ here _____

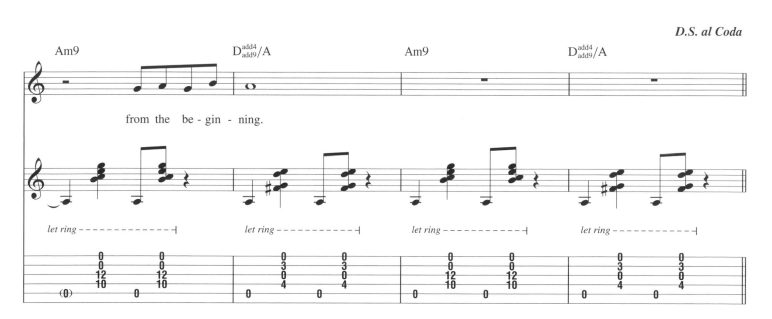

D.S. al Coda

Am9   D$_{add9}^{add4}$/A   Am9   D$_{add9}^{add4}$/A

from the be - gin - ning.

Coda

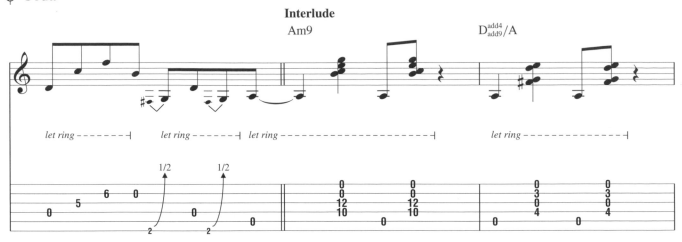

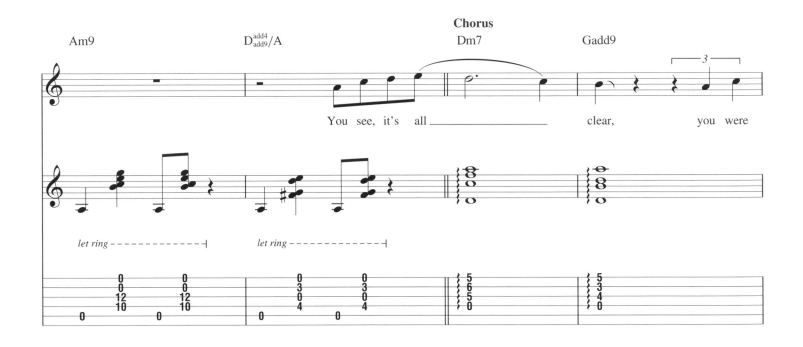

You see, it's all _____ clear, you were

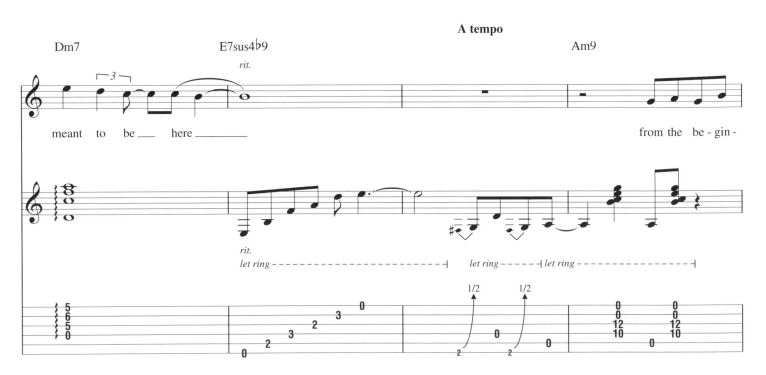

meant to be here _____ from the be-gin-

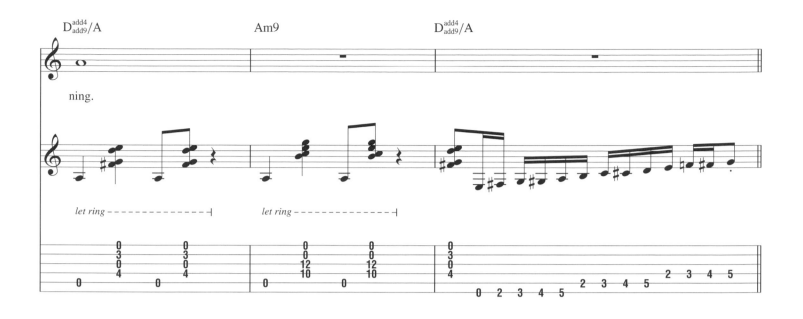

Guitar Solo

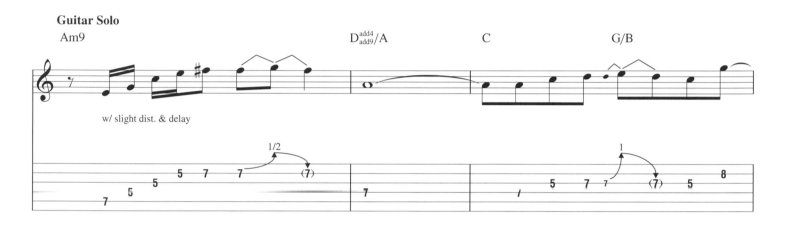

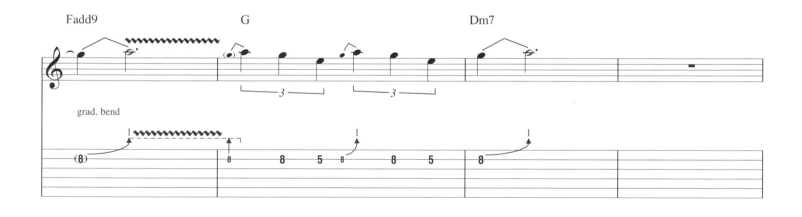

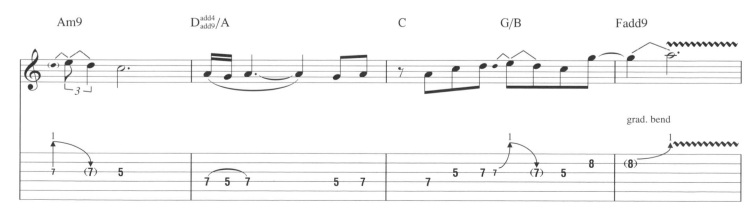

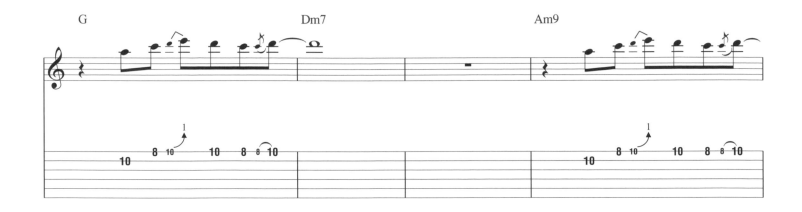

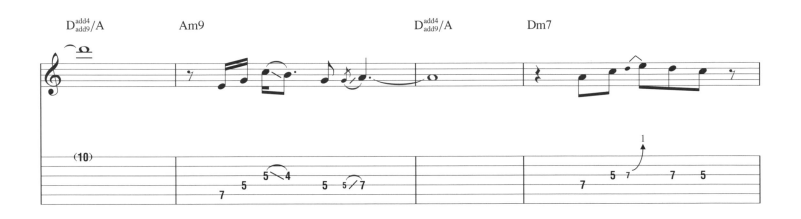

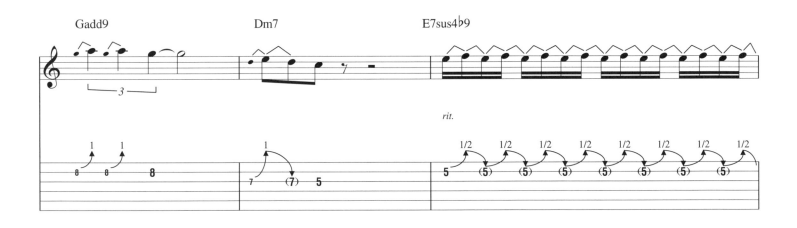

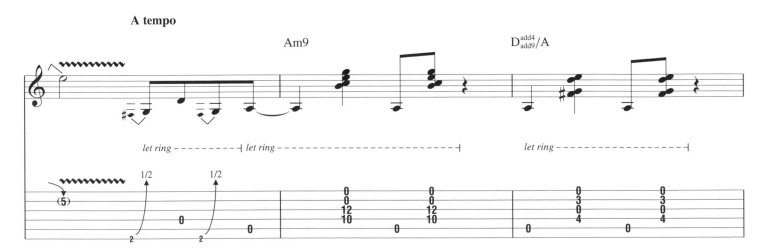

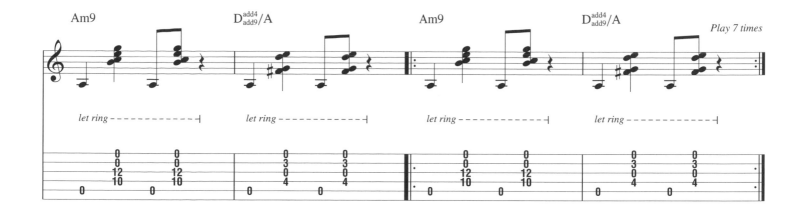

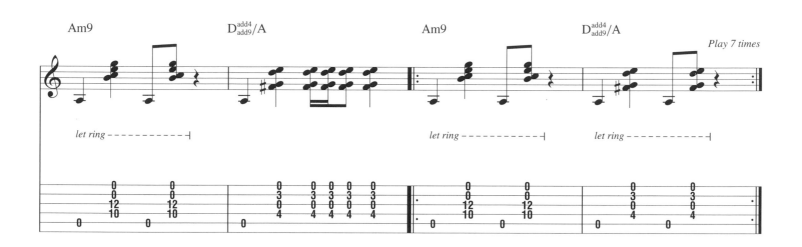

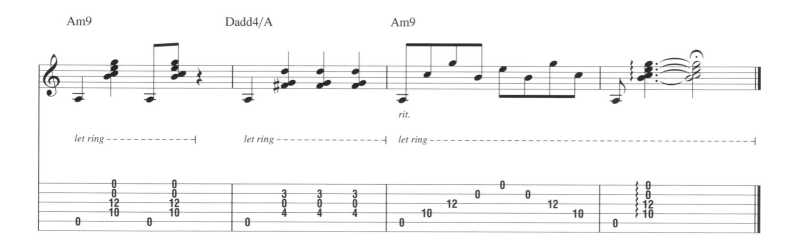

Additional Lyrics

2. Maybe I might have changed
   And not been so cruel.
   Not been such a fool.
   Whatever was done is done.
   I just can't recall.
   It doesn't matter at all.

Locomotive Breath

Words and Music by Ian Anderson

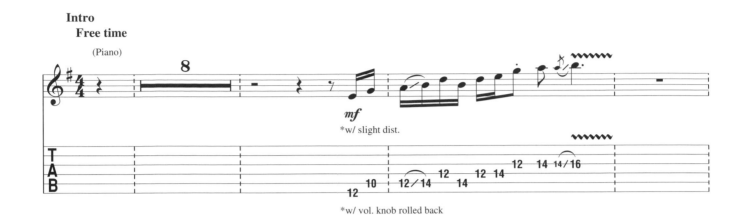

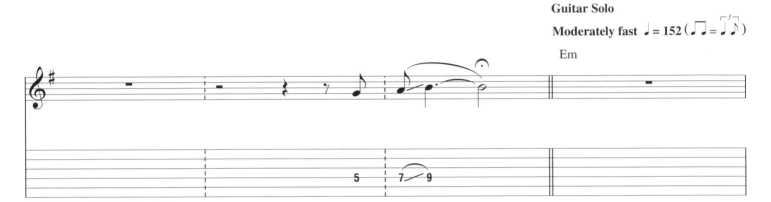

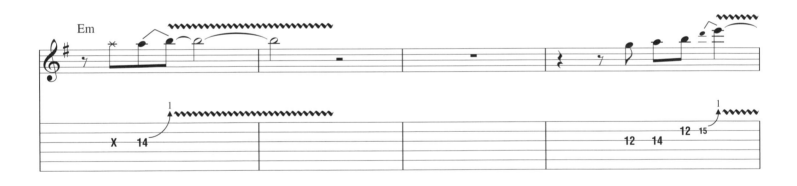

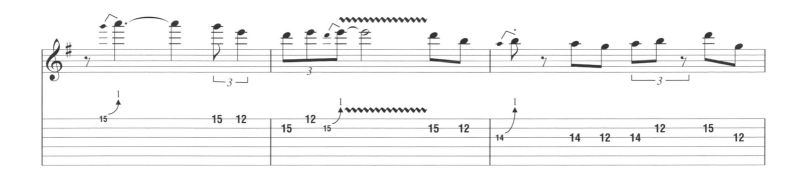

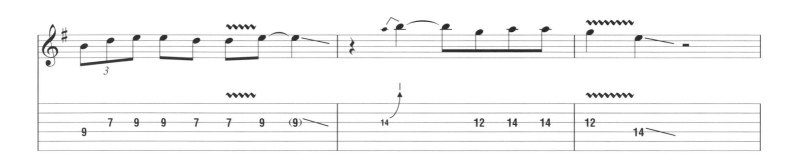

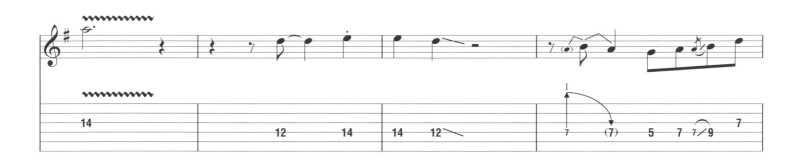

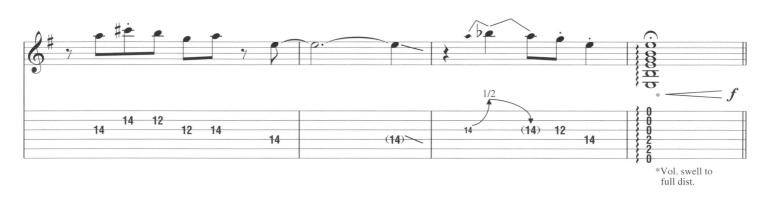

*Vol. swell to
full dist.

Intro
Slower ♩ = 120 (♫ = ♪♪)

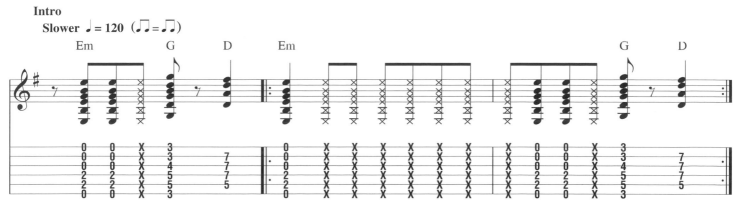

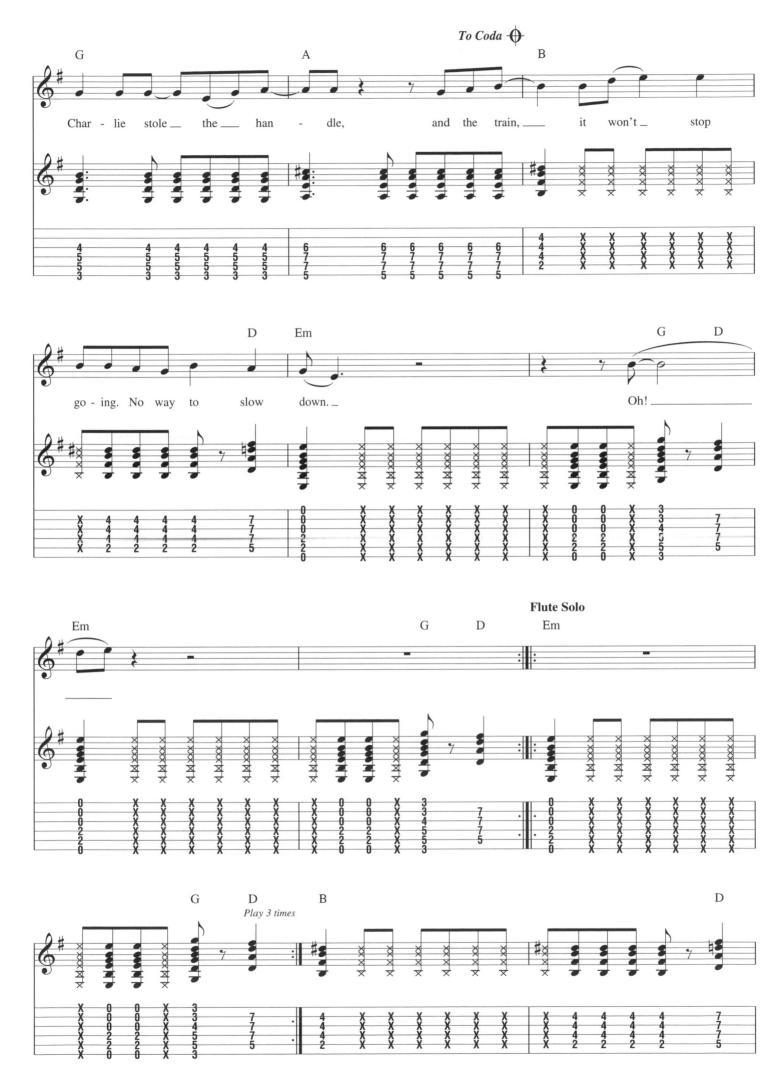

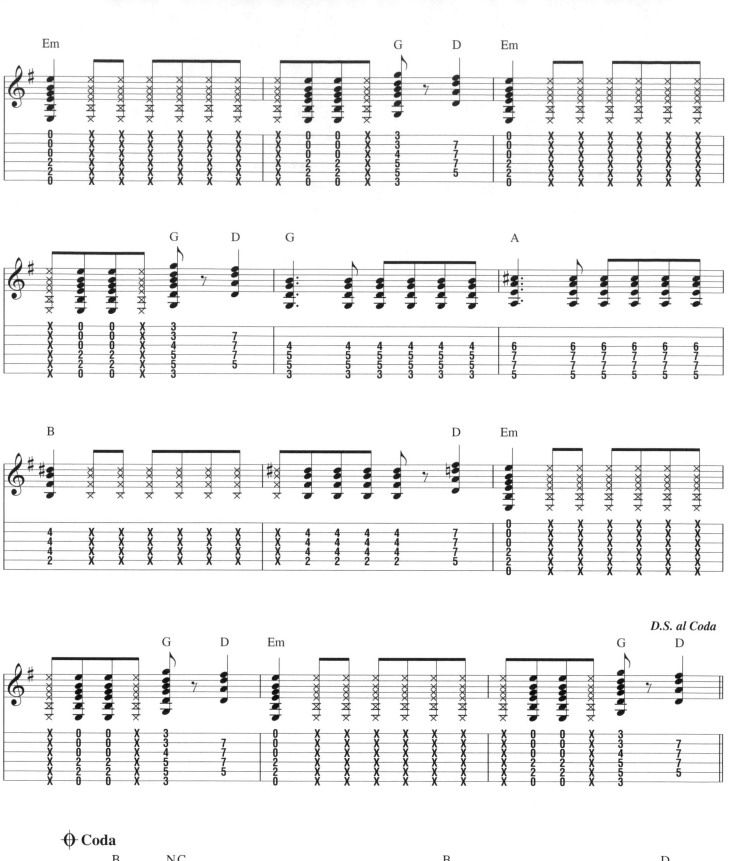

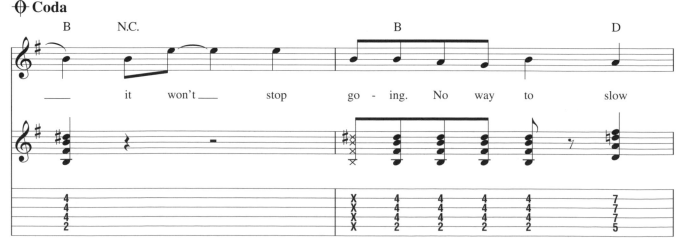

it won't ___ stop go - ing. No way to slow

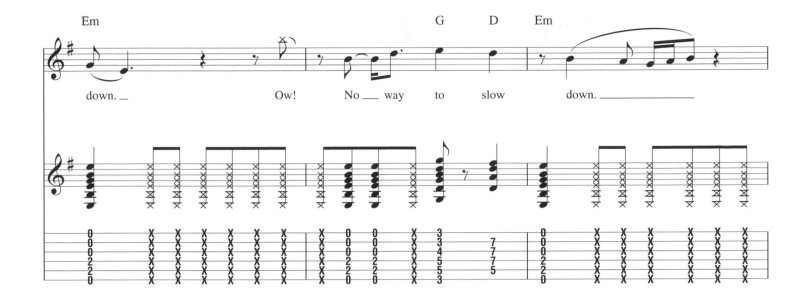

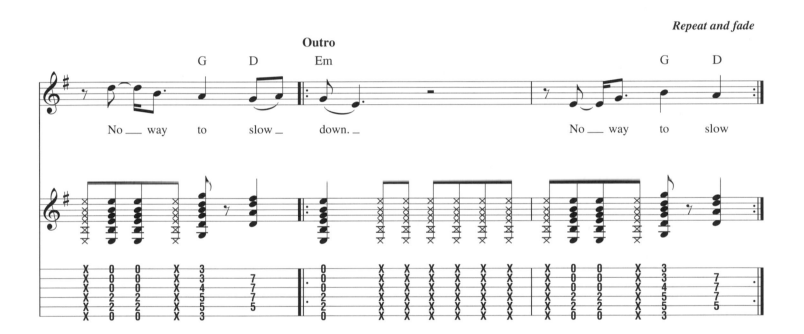

Additional Lyrics

2. He sees his children jumping off
   At stations, one by one.
   His woman and his best friend,
   In bed and having fun.
   Oh, he's crawling down the corridor
   On his hands and knees.
   Old Charlie stole the handle,
   And the train it won't stop going.
   No way to slow down. A-hey. Hey.

3. He hears the silence howling,
   Catches angels as they fall.
   And the all-time winner
   Has got him by the balls.
   Oh, he picks up Gideon's Bible,
   Open at page one.
   I thank God he stole the handle,
   And the train, it won't stop going.
   No way to slow down. Ow!
   No way to slow down.

Owner of a Lonely Heart

Words and Music by Trevor Horn, Jon Anderson, Trevor Rabin and Chris Squire

*Octaver set for 1 octave above.

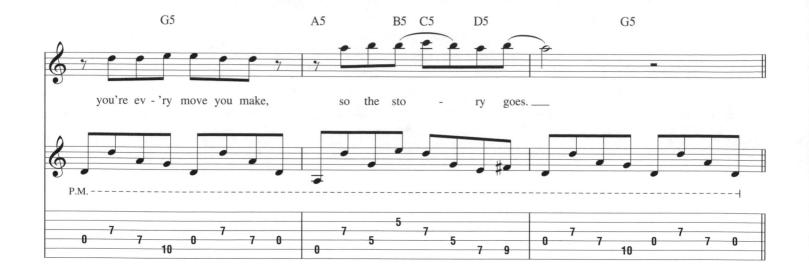

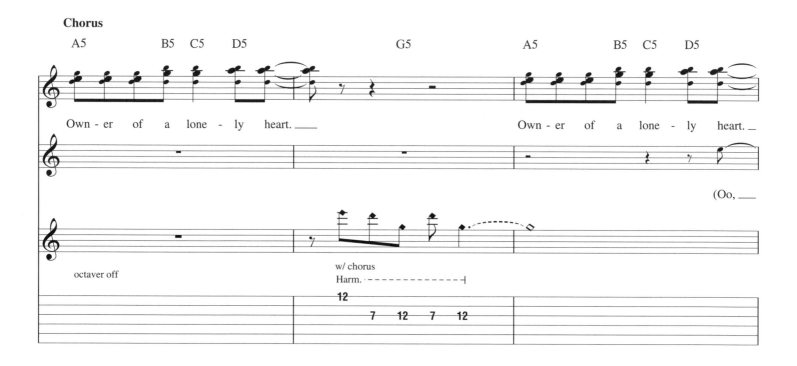

Chorus

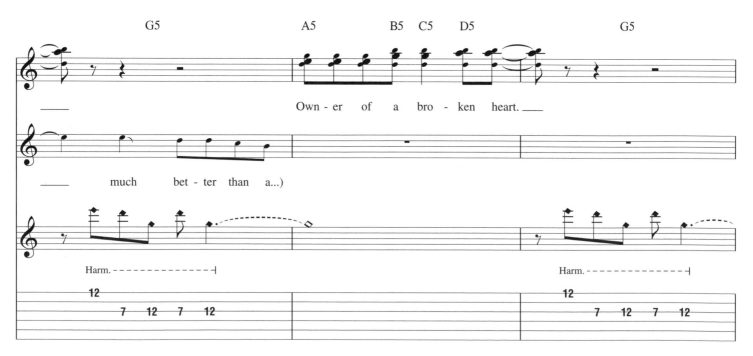

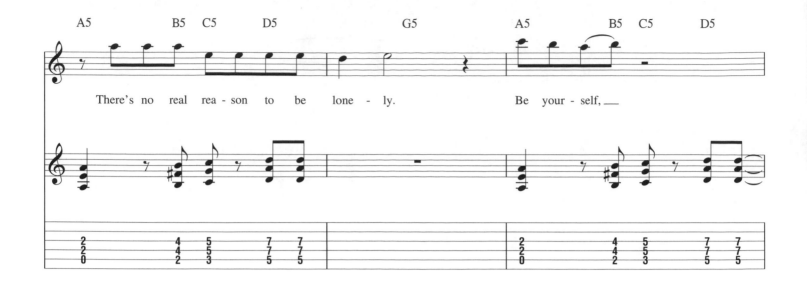

There's no real rea-son to be lone-ly. Be your-self, ___

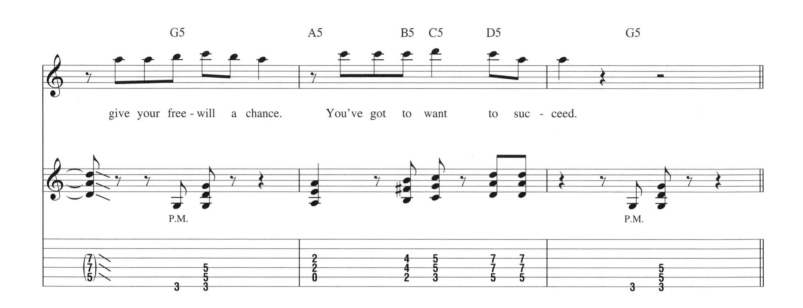

give your free-will a chance. You've got to want to suc-ceed.

P.M.

P.M.

Chorus

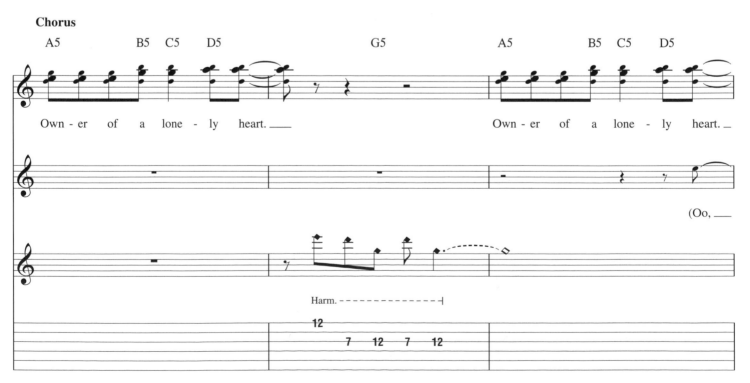

Own-er of a lone-ly heart. ___ Own-er of a lone-ly heart. ___

(Oo, ___

Harm.

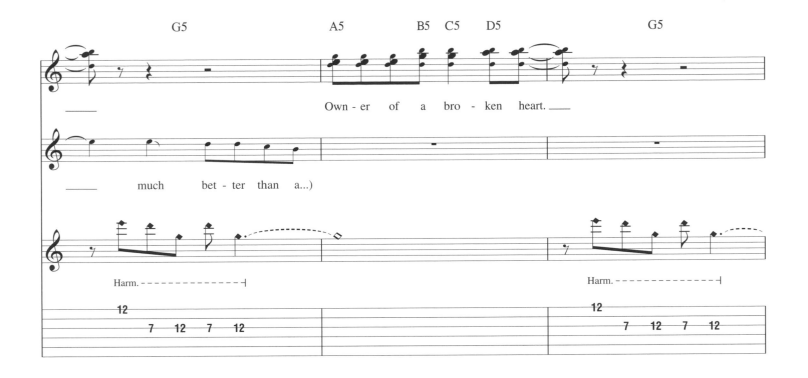

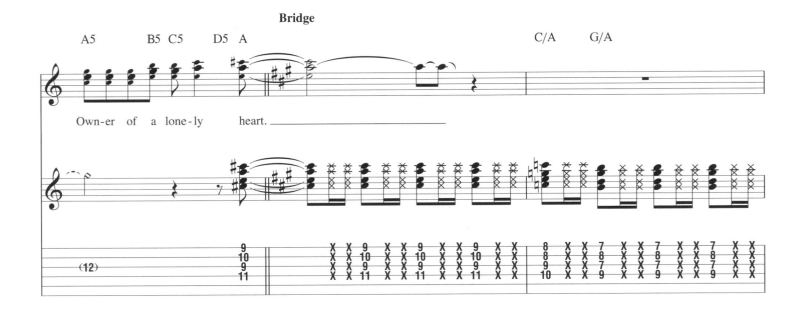

Bridge

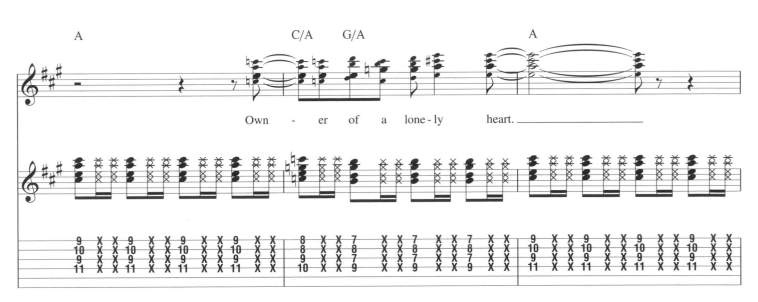

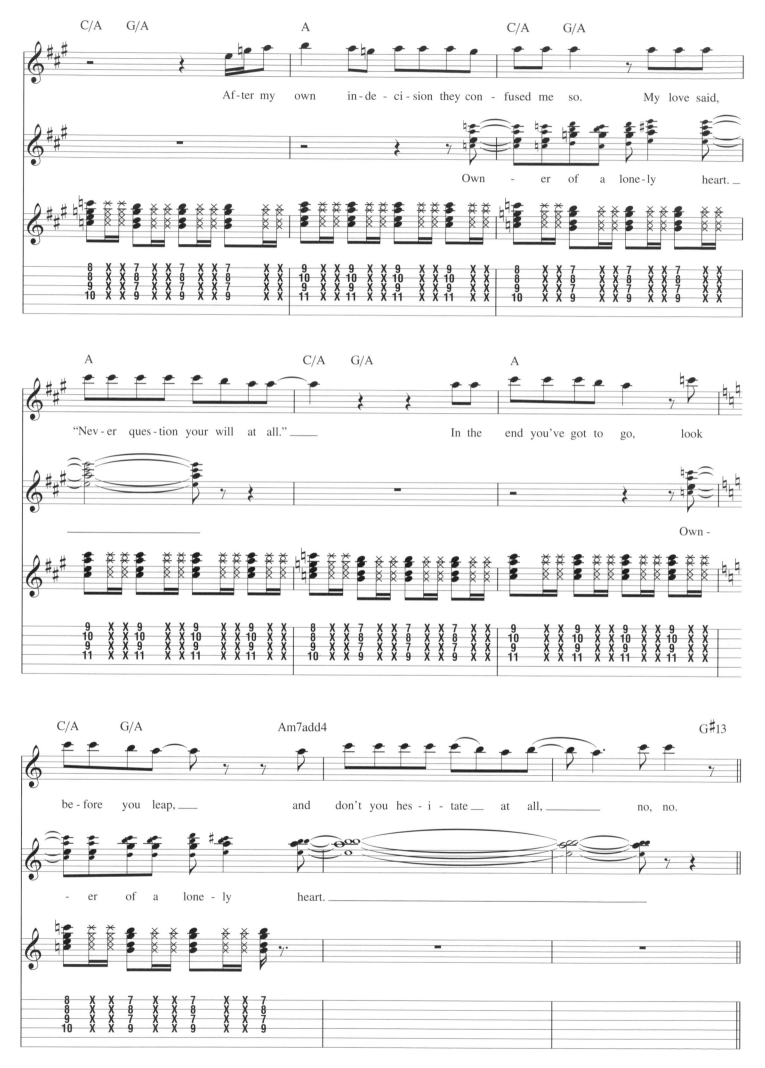

Breakdown

Gtr. tacet

*Set to harmonize one octave below and a fifth above.

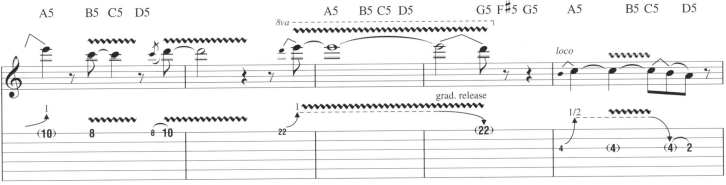

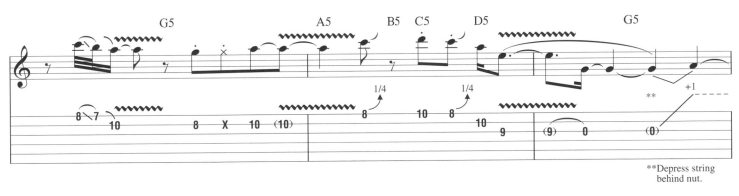

**Depress string
behind nut.

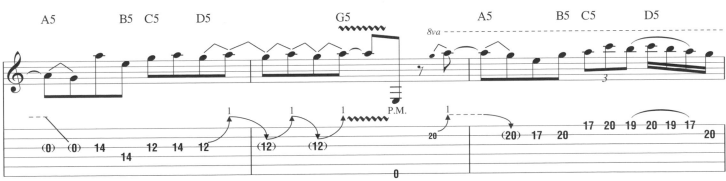

Interlude

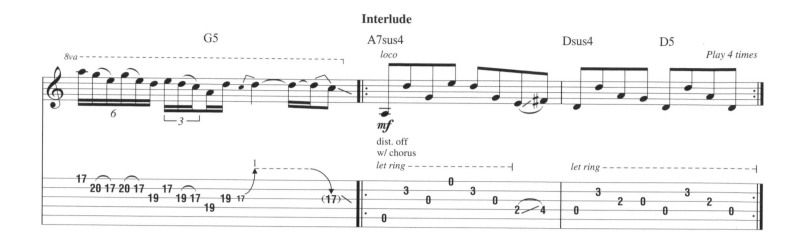

Chorus

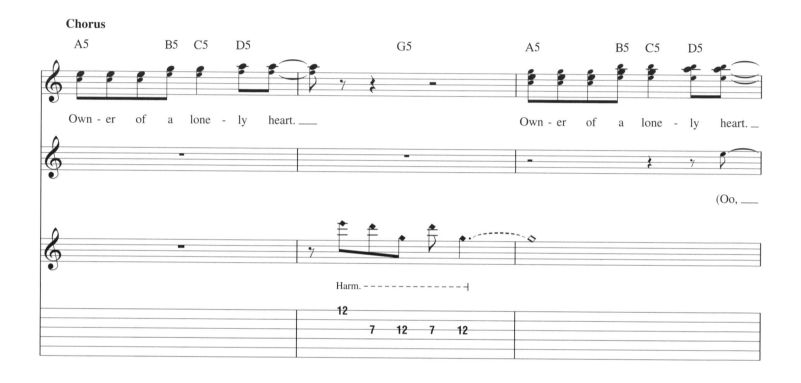

Own - er of a lone - ly heart. ___

Own - er of a lone - ly heart. ___

(Oo, ___

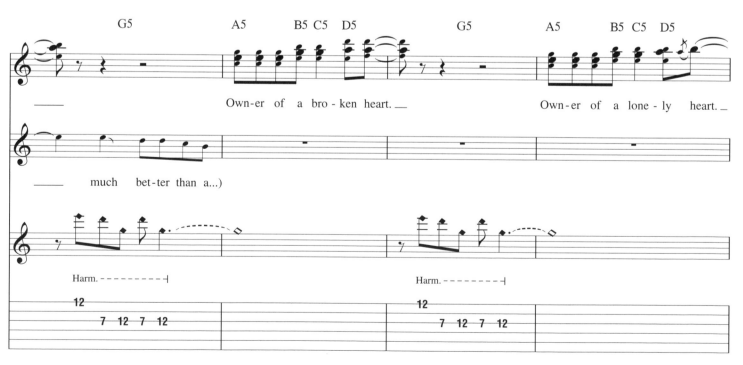

___ much bet - ter than a...)

Own - er of a bro - ken heart. ___

Own - er of a lone - ly heart. ___

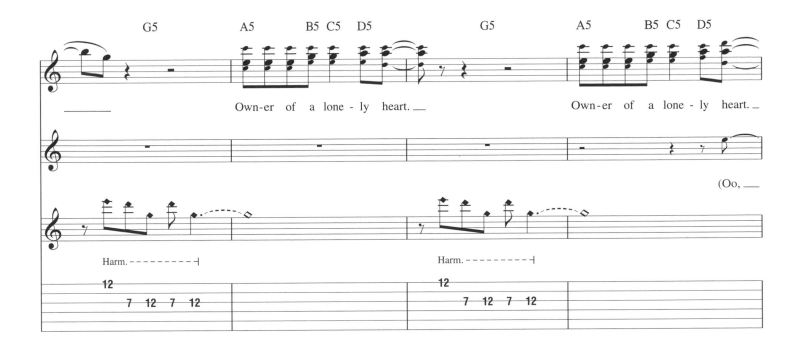

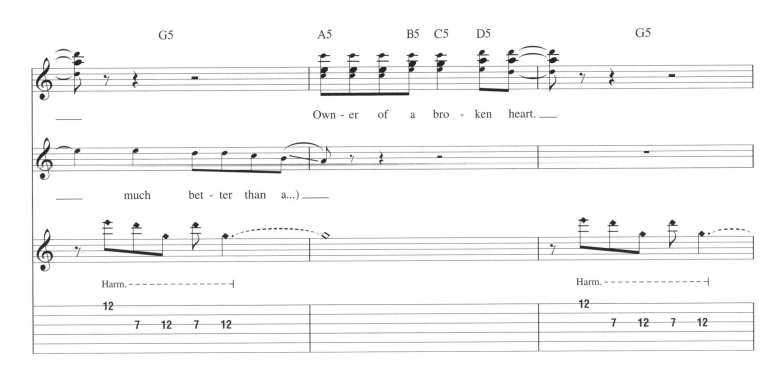

Outro-Bridge

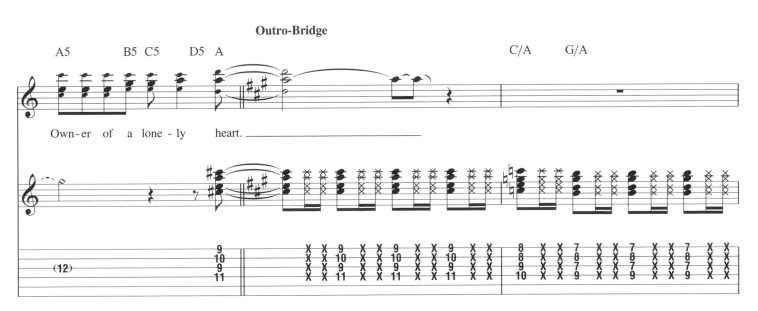

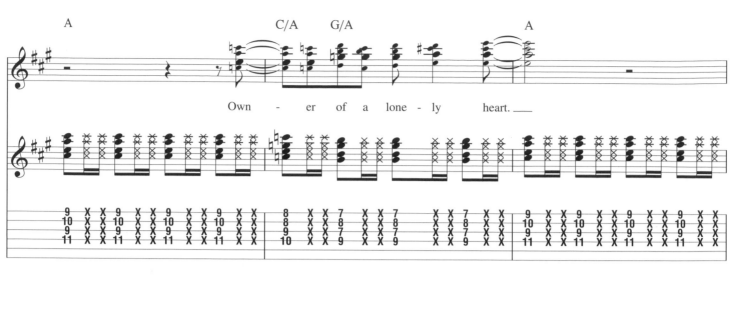

Own - er of a lone - ly heart. ___

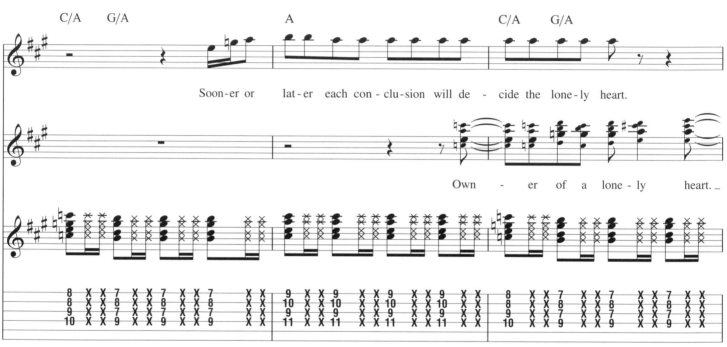

Soon-er or lat-er each con-clu-sion will de - cide the lone-ly heart.

Own - er of a lone - ly heart. _

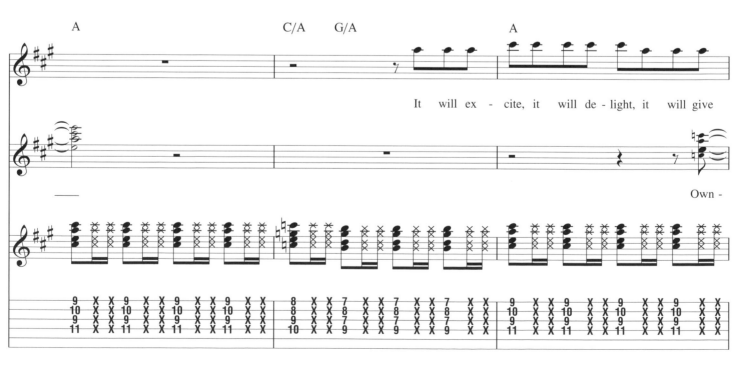

It will ex - cite, it will de - light, it will give

Own -

Turn It On Again

Words and Music by Tony Banks, Phil Collins and Mike Rutherford

Intro
Moderately ♩ = 126

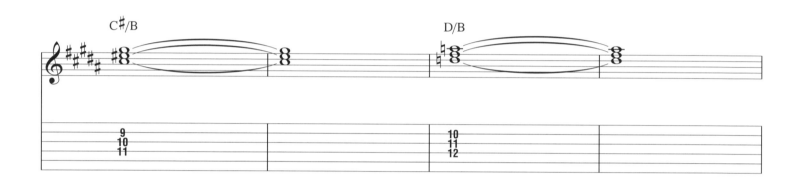

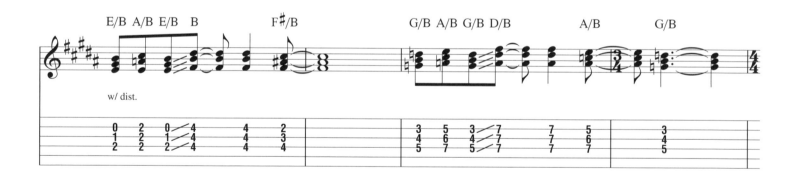

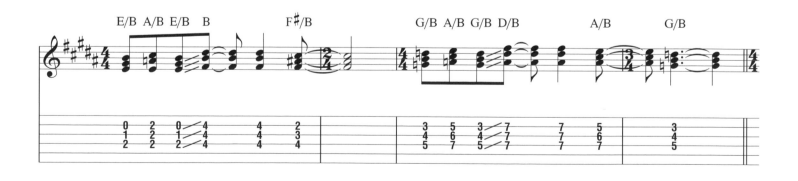

Verse

1. All I need is a T_____ V____ show, _____ that ___ and the

ra - di - o. Down ____ on my luck a - gain, _____

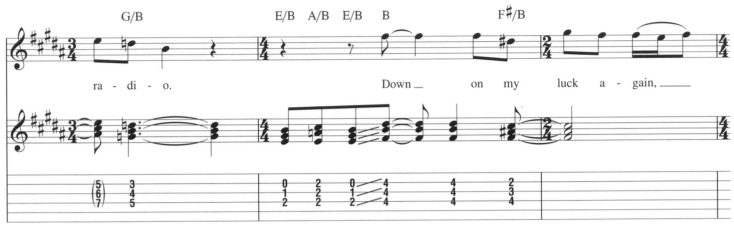

𝄋 **Pre-Chorus**

down _____ on my luck a - gain. I can show __ you, I ___

*2nd time, omit ties.

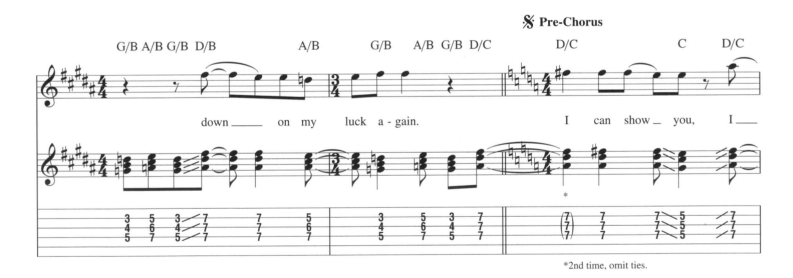

____ can show __ you __ some of the peo - ple in my ____ life.

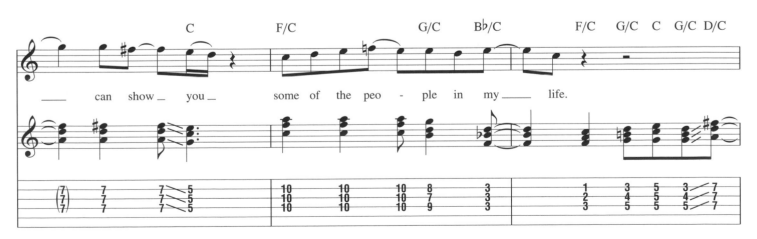

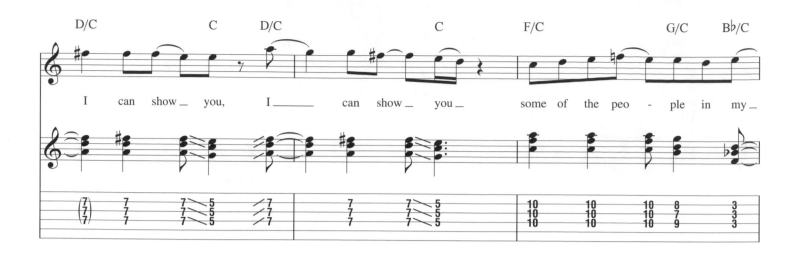

I can show you, I can show you some of the peo - ple in my

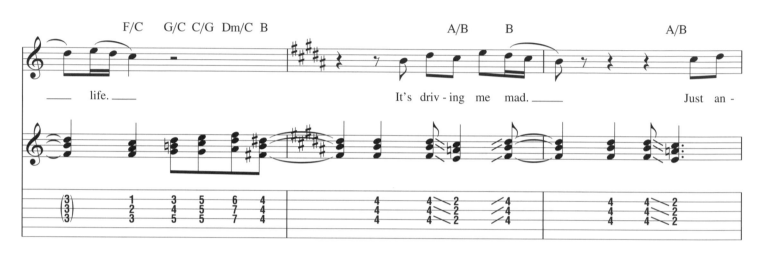

life. It's driv - ing me mad. Just an -

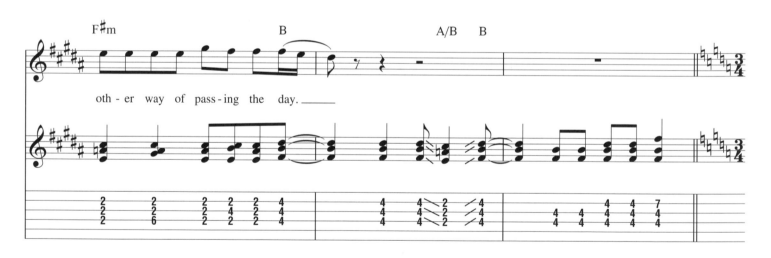

oth - er way of pass - ing the day.

Chorus

I, I,

get so lone - ly when she's____ not there.____   I,____

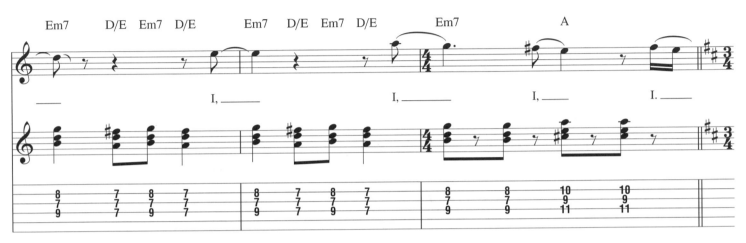

____   I,____   I,____   I,____   I.____

Interlude

To Coda ⊕

Verse

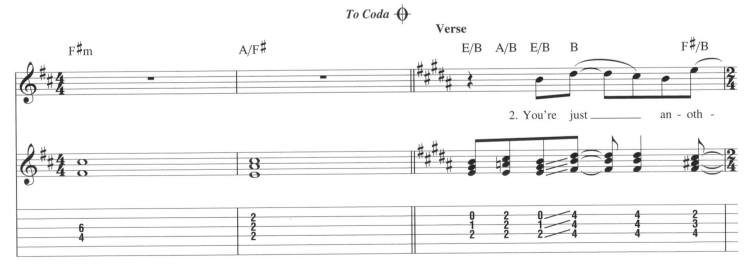

2. You're just_____ an - oth -

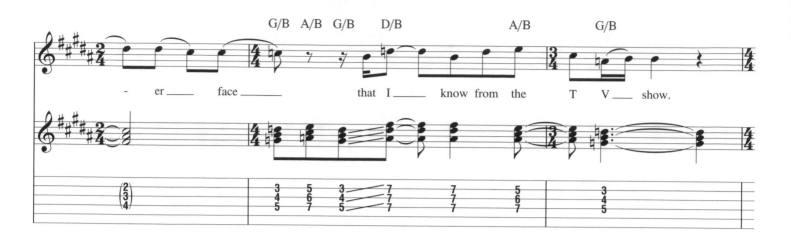

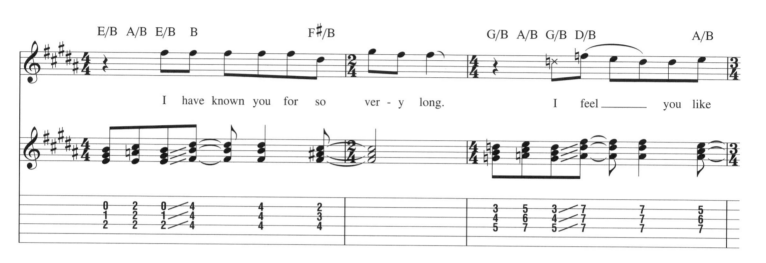

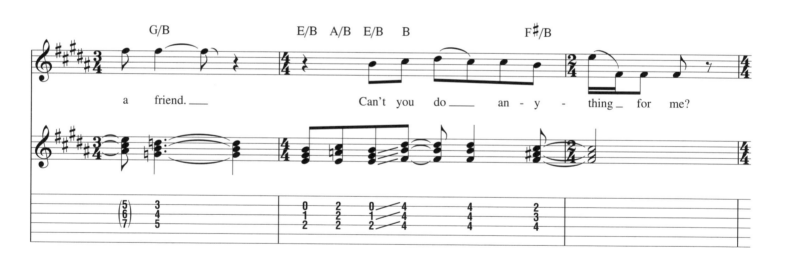

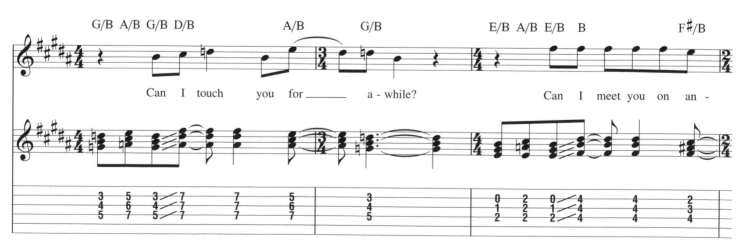

oth - er day? ___ And we ___ will fly a - way. ___

Coda

Outro

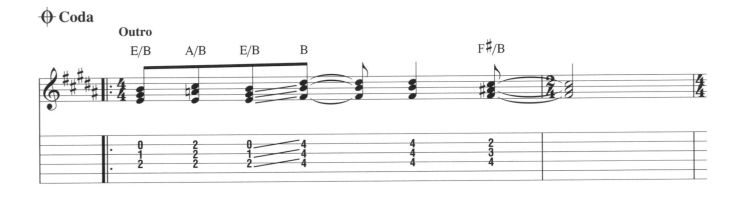

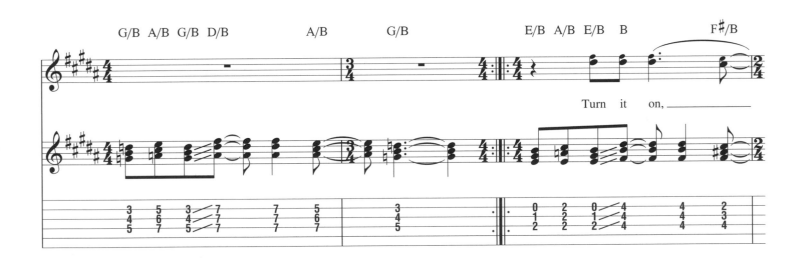

Turn it on, ___

turn it on, turn it on a - gain.

21st Century Schizoid Man

Words and Music by Robert Fripp, Michael Giles, Greg Lake, Ian McDonald and Peter Sinfield

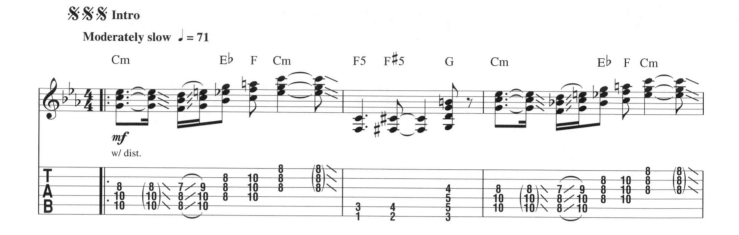

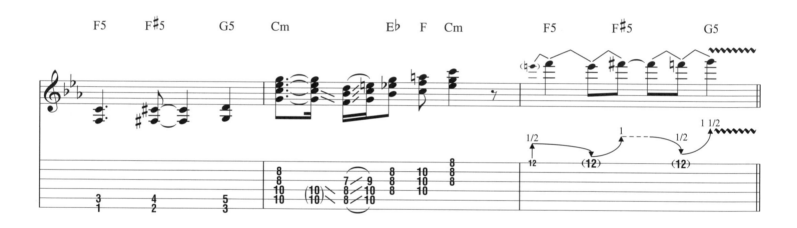

At par - a - noi - a's poi - son door. Twen - ty - first Cen - t'ry Schiz - oid Man.

*T = Thumb on 6th string.

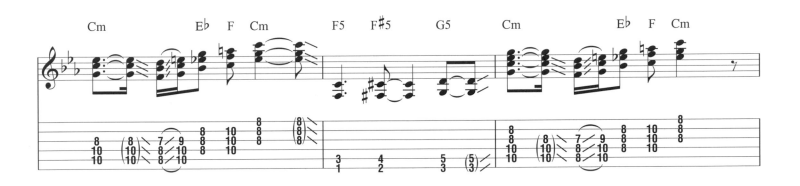

Cm   Eb F Cm   F5   F#5   G5   Cm   Eb F Cm

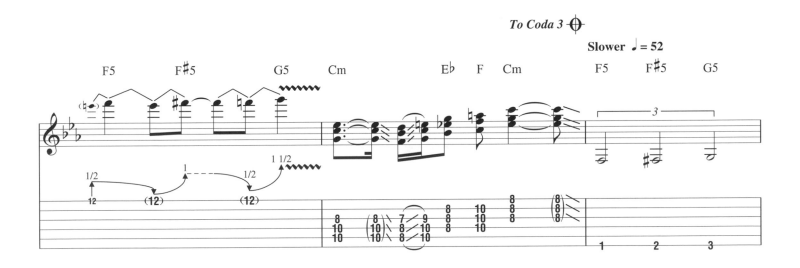

To Coda 3 ✛

Slower ♩ = 52

F5   F#5   G5   Cm   Eb F Cm   F5   F#5   G5

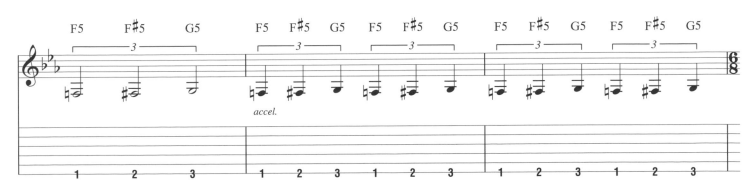

F5   F#5   G5   F5   F#5   G5   F5   F#5   G5   F5   F#5   G5   F5   F#5   G5

accel.

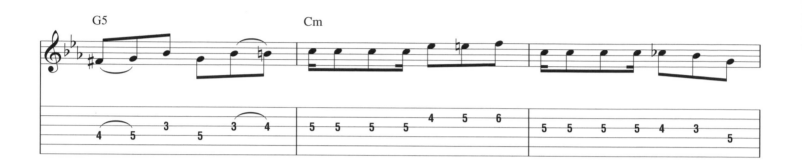

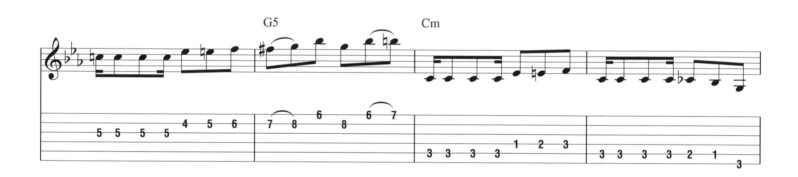

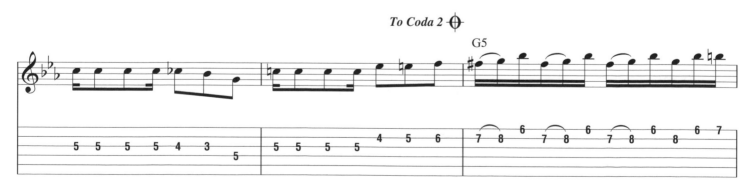

2nd time, substitute Fill 1

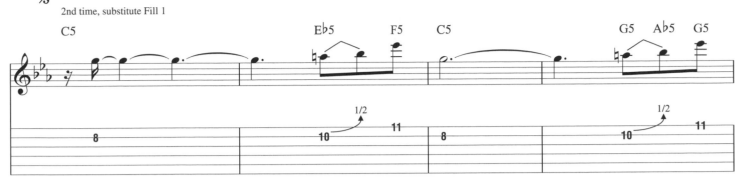

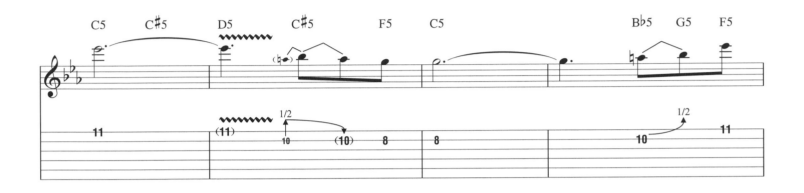

To Coda 1 ⊕

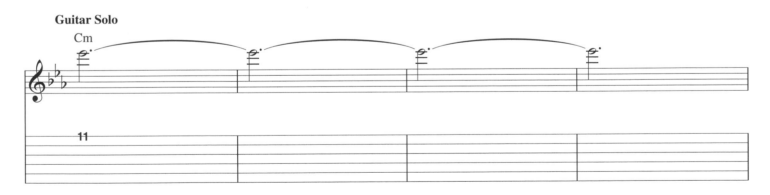

Guitar Solo

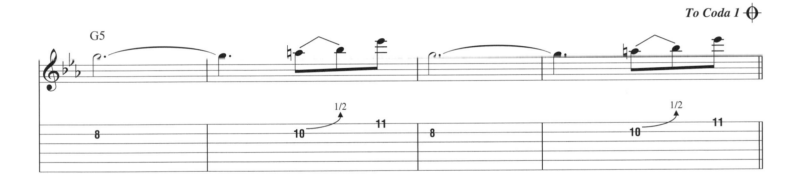

Fill 1

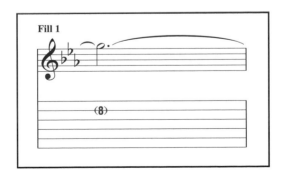

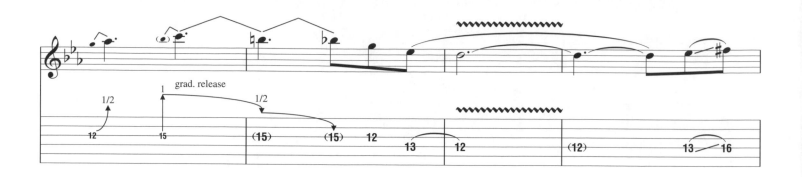

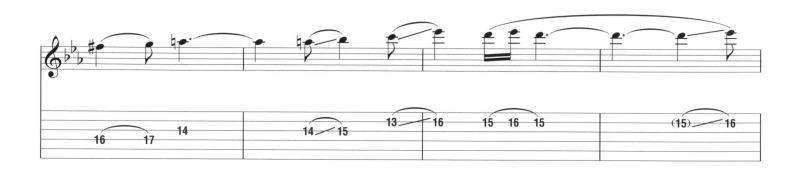

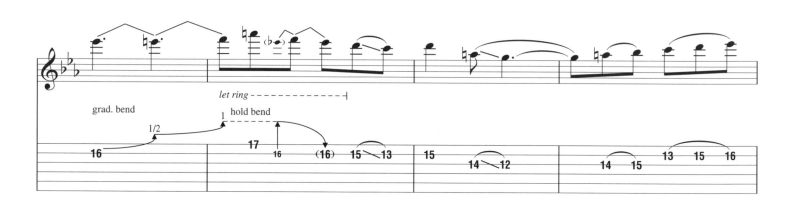

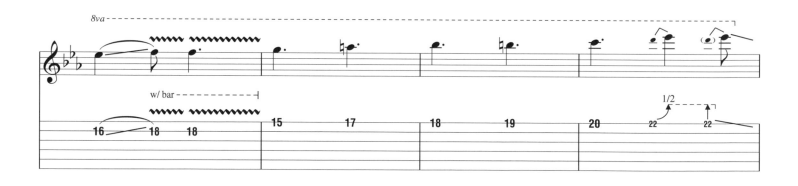

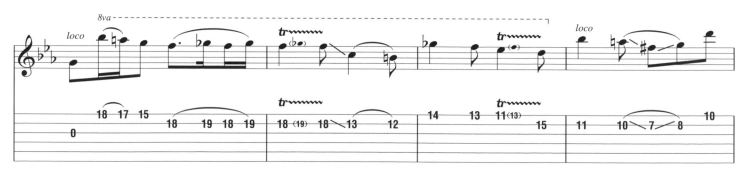

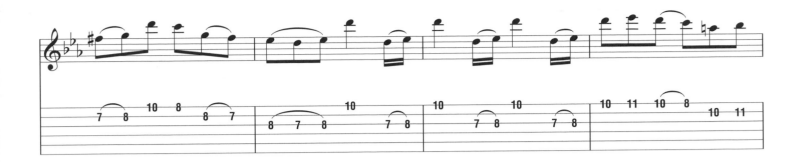

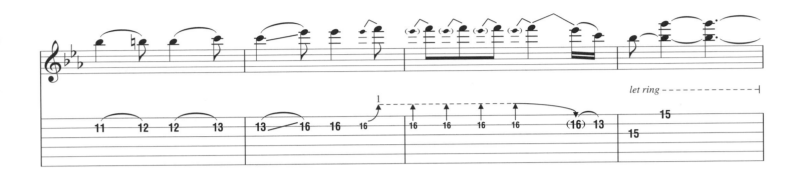

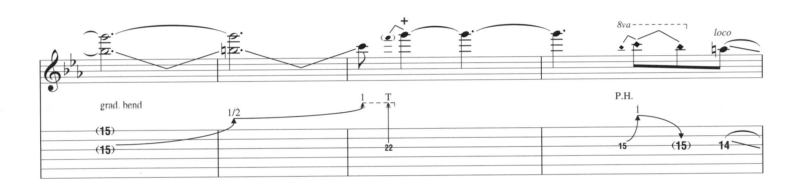

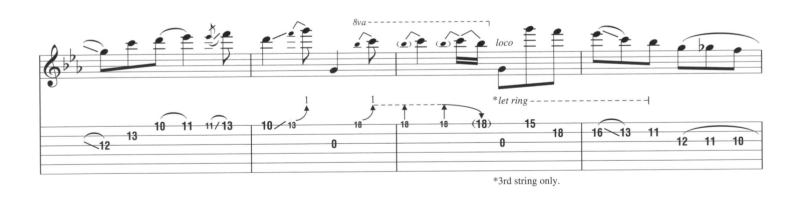

*3rd string only.

Saxophone Solo

Cm

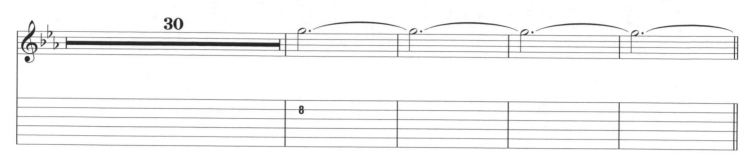

Coda 1

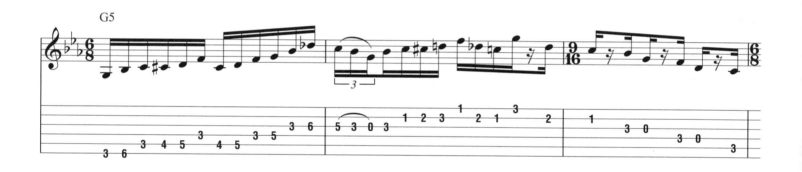

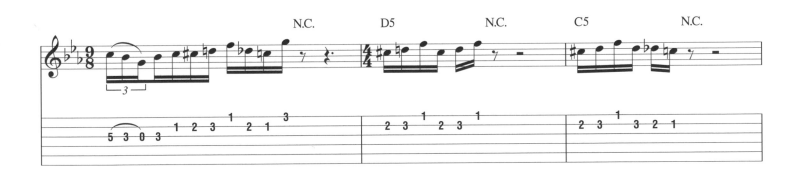

D.S.S. al Coda 2

⊕ Coda 2

Gm

D.S.S.S. al Coda 3
(no repeat)

⊕ Coda 3

Slower ♩ = 52

F5　F#5　G5　F5　F#5　G5　F5　F#5　G5　F5　F#5　G5

Free time

F5　F#5　G5　F5　F#5　G5　F5　F#5　G5　F5　F#5　G5

(Random strumming & noise)

Additional Lyrics

2. Blood rack, barbed wire.
   Politicians' funeral pyre.
   Innocents raped with napalm fire.

3. Death seed, blind man's greed.
   Poets starving, children bleed.
   Nothing he's got he really needs.

The Wall

Words and Music by Kerry Livgren and Steve Walsh

Intro
Moderately slow ♩ = 88

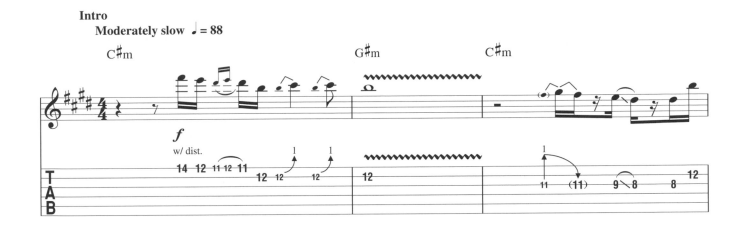

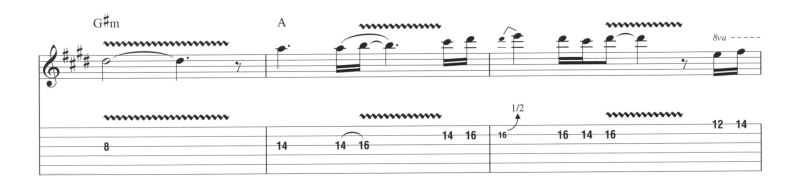

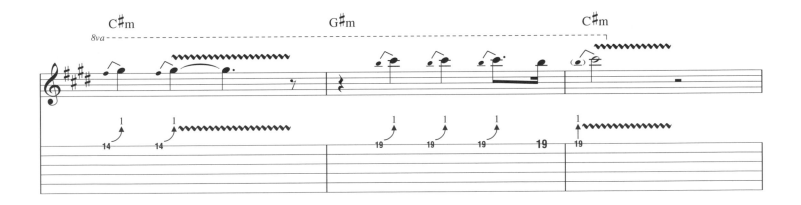

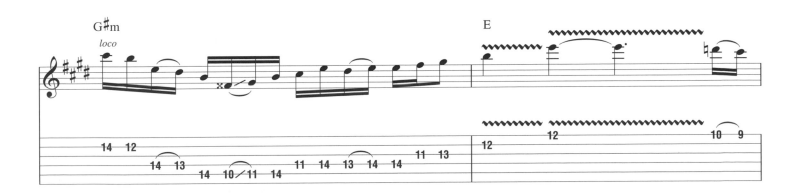

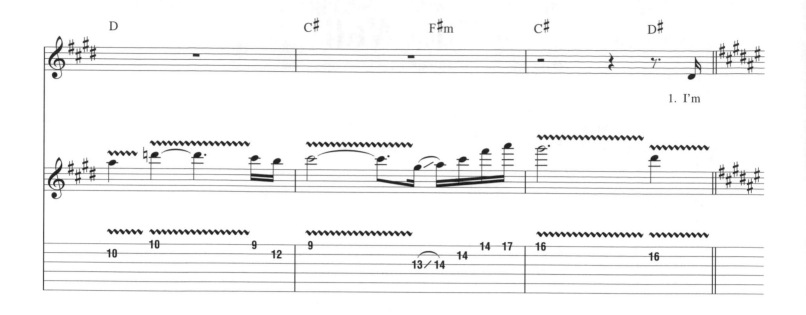

Verse

wo - ven in ___ a fan - ta - sy, I can't ___ be - lieve ___ the things ___ I ___ see. ___ The

path that I ___ have cho - sen ___ now has led me to a wall, ___ and

with each pass - ing day I feel ___ a lit - tle more ___ like some - thing dear ___ was

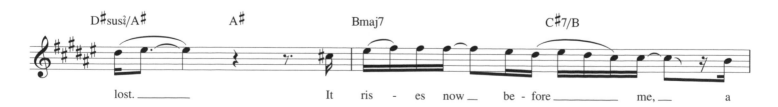

lost. ___ It ris - es now ___ be - fore ___ me, ___ a

dark __ and si - lent bar - ri - er ____ be - tween ____ all I __

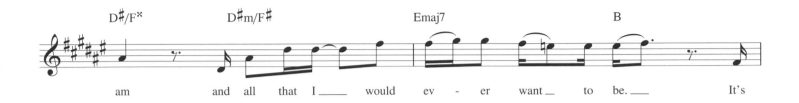

am and all that I ____ would ev - er want __ to be. ____ It's

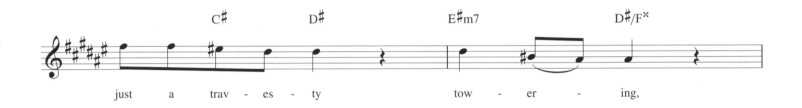

just a trav - es - ty tow - er - ing,

mark - ing off ____ the bound - a - ries ____ my spir - it would e -

rase.   2. To pass be - yond __ is what I seek.   I

*Violin arr. for gtr., next 17 meas.

fear _ that I _ may be _ too _ weak. _ And those _ are few _ who've seen it through to

glimpse the oth - er side. _____ The prom-ised land _ is wait-ing like _ a

maid - en that is soon _ to be _ a bride. _____ The

mo - ment is _____ a mas - ter-piece, the weight _ of in - de - ci-sion's in the

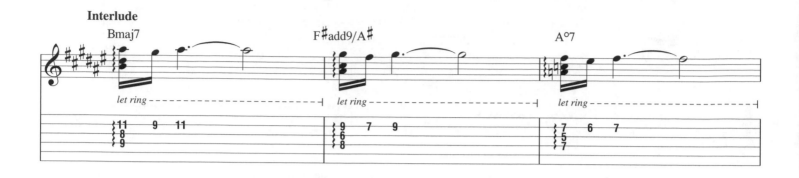

Guitar Solo

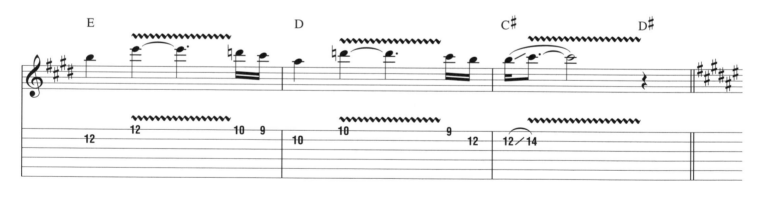

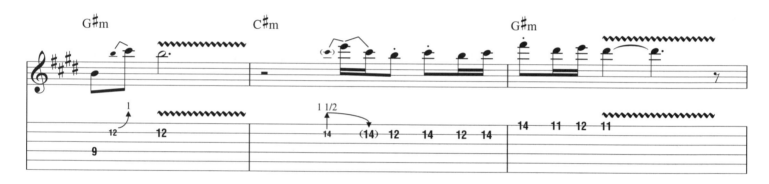

Verse

3. Gold and di - 'monds cast __ a spell, __ it's not for me, __ I know it well. __ The

*Violin arr. for gtr., next 17 meas.

68

am and all that I ____ was ev - er meant to be ____

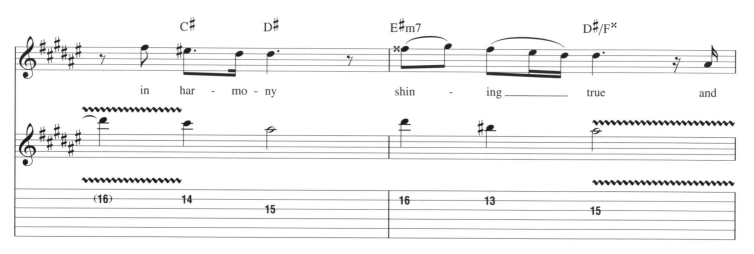

in har - mo - ny shin - ing ____ true and

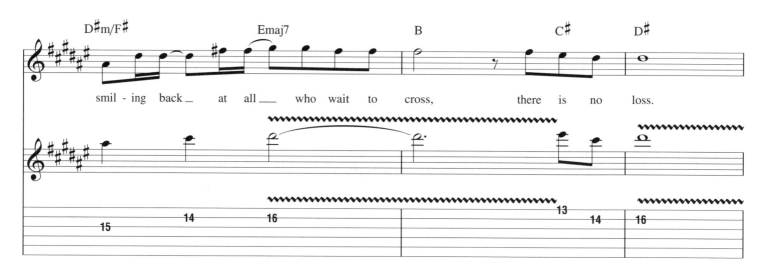

smil - ing back ___ at all ___ who wait to cross, there is no loss.

Outro

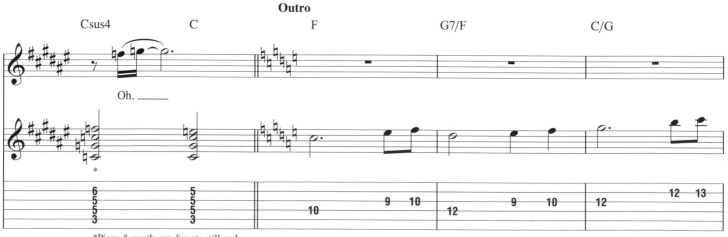

Oh. ____

*Piano & synth. arr. for gtr., till end.

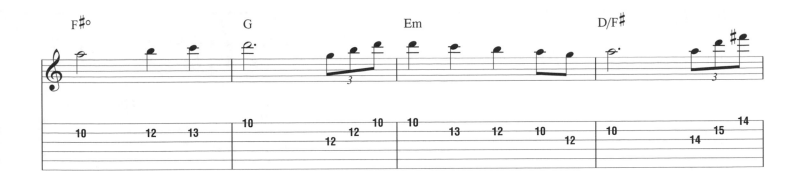

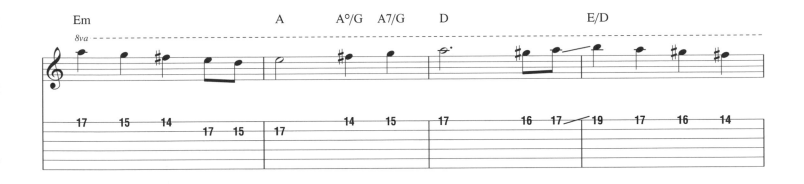

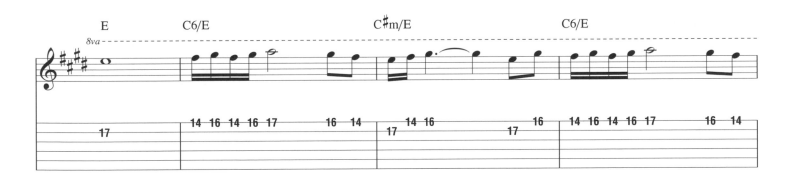

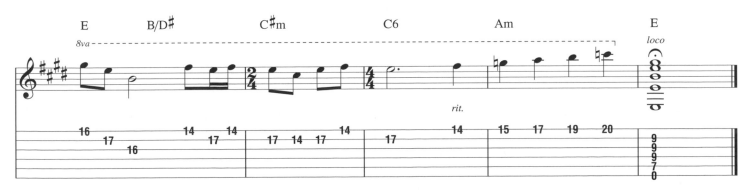

HAL•LEONARD GUITAR PLAY•ALONG

This series will help you play your favorite songs quickly and easily. Just follow the tab and listen to the CD to hear how the guitar should sound, and then play along using the separate backing tracks. Mac or PC users can also slow down the tempo without changing pitch by using the CD in their computer. The melody and lyrics are included in the book so that you can sing or simply follow along.

INCLUDES TAB

VOL. 1 – ROCK	00699570 / $16.99
VOL. 2 – ACOUSTIC	00699569 / $16.95
VOL. 3 – HARD ROCK	00699573 / $16.95
VOL. 4 – POP/ROCK	00699571 / $16.99
VOL. 5 – MODERN ROCK	00699574 / $16.99
VOL. 6 – '90s ROCK	00699572 / $16.99
VOL. 7 – BLUES	00699575 / $16.95
VOL. 8 – ROCK	00699585 / $12.95
VOL. 9 – PUNK ROCK	00699576 / $14.95
VOL. 10 – ACOUSTIC	00699586 / $16.95
VOL. 11 – EARLY ROCK	00699579 / $14.95
VOL. 12 – POP/ROCK	00699587 / $14.95
VOL. 13 – FOLK ROCK	00699581 / $14.95
VOL. 14 – BLUES ROCK	00699582 / $16.95
VOL. 15 – R&B	00699583 / $14.95
VOL. 16 – JAZZ	00699584 / $15.95
VOL. 17 – COUNTRY	00699588 / $15.95
VOL. 18 – ACOUSTIC ROCK	00699577 / $15.95
VOL. 19 – SOUL	00699578 / $14.95
VOL. 20 – ROCKABILLY	00699580 / $14.95
VOL. 21 – YULETIDE	00699602 / $14.95
VOL. 22 – CHRISTMAS	00699600 / $15.95
VOL. 23 – SURF	00699635 / $14.95
VOL. 24 – ERIC CLAPTON	00699649 / $16.95
VOL. 25 – LENNON & McCARTNEY	00699642 / $14.95
VOL. 26 – ELVIS PRESLEY	00699643 / $14.95
VOL. 27 – DAVID LEE ROTH	00699645 / $16.95
VOL. 28 – GREG KOCH	00699646 / $14.95
VOL. 29 – BOB SEGER	00699647 / $14.95
VOL. 30 – KISS	00699644 / $16.99
VOL. 31 – CHRISTMAS HITS	00699652 / $14.95
VOL. 32 – THE OFFSPRING	00699653 / $14.95
VOL. 33 – ACOUSTIC CLASSICS	00699656 / $16.95
VOL. 34 – CLASSIC ROCK	00699658 / $16.95
VOL. 35 – HAIR METAL	00699660 / $16.95
VOL. 36 – SOUTHERN ROCK	00699661 / $16.95
VOL. 37 – ACOUSTIC METAL	00699662 / $16.95
VOL. 38 – BLUES	00699663 / $16.95
VOL. 39 – '80s METAL	00699664 / $16.99
VOL. 40 – INCUBUS	00699668 / $17.95
VOL. 41 – ERIC CLAPTON	00699669 / $16.95
VOL. 42 – CHART HITS	00699670 / $16.95
VOL. 43 – LYNYRD SKYNYRD	00699681 / $17.95

VOL. 44 – JAZZ	00699689 / $14.95
VOL. 45 – TV THEMES	00699718 / $14.95
VOL. 46 – MAINSTREAM ROCK	00699722 / $16.95
VOL. 47 – HENDRIX SMASH HITS	00699723 / $19.95
VOL. 48 – AEROSMITH CLASSICS	00699724 / $16.99
VOL. 49 – STEVIE RAY VAUGHAN	00699725 / $16.95
VOL. 50 – NÜ METAL	00699726 / $14.95
VOL. 51 – ALTERNATIVE '90s	00699727 / $12.95
VOL. 52 – FUNK	00699728 / $14.95
VOL. 53 – DISCO	00699729 / $14.99
VOL. 54 – HEAVY METAL	00699730 / $14.95
VOL. 55 – POP METAL	00699731 / $14.95
VOL. 56 – FOO FIGHTERS	00699749 / $14.95
VOL. 57 – SYSTEM OF A DOWN	00699751 / $14.95
VOL. 58 – BLINK-182	00699772 / $14.95
VOL. 59 – GODSMACK	00699773 / $14.95
VOL. 60 – 3 DOORS DOWN	00699774 / $14.95
VOL. 61 – SLIPKNOT	00699775 / $14.95
VOL. 62 – CHRISTMAS CAROLS	00699798 / $12.95
VOL. 63 – CREEDENCE CLEARWATER REVIVAL	00699802 / $16.99
VOL. 64 – THE ULTIMATE OZZY OSBOURNE	00699803 / $16.99
VOL. 65 – THE DOORS	00699806 / $16.99
VOL. 66 – THE ROLLING STONES	00699807 / $16.95
VOL. 67 – BLACK SABBATH	00699808 / $16.99
VOL. 68 – PINK FLOYD – DARK SIDE OF THE MOON	00699809 / $16.99
VOL. 69 – ACOUSTIC FAVORITES	00699810 / $14.95
VOL. 70 – OZZY OSBOURNE	00699805 / $16.99
VOL. 71 – CHRISTIAN ROCK	00699824 / $14.95
VOL. 72 – ACOUSTIC '90s	00699827 / $14.95
VOL. 73 – BLUESY ROCK	00699829 / $16.99
VOL. 74 – PAUL BALOCHE	00699831 / $14.95
VOL. 75 – TOM PETTY	00699882 / $16.99
VOL. 76 – COUNTRY HITS	00699884 / $14.95
VOL. 78 – NIRVANA	00700132 / $14.95
VOL. 80 – ACOUSTIC ANTHOLOGY	00700175 / $19.95
VOL. 81 – ROCK ANTHOLOGY	00700176 / $22.99

VOL. 82 – EASY SONGS	00700177 / $12.99
VOL. 83 – THREE CHORD SONGS	00700178 / $14.99
VOL. 84 – STEELY DAN	00700200 / $16.99
VOL. 85 – THE POLICE	00700269 / $16.99
VOL. 86 – BOSTON	00700465 / $16.99
VOL. 87 – ACOUSTIC WOMEN	00700763 / $14.99
VOL. 88 – GRUNGE	00700467 / $16.99
VOL. 91 – BLUES INSTRUMENTALS	00700505 / $14.99
VOL. 92 – EARLY ROCK INSTRUMENTALS	00700506 / $12.99
VOL. 93 – ROCK INSTRUMENTALS	00700507 / $14.99
VOL. 96 – THIRD DAY	00700560 / $14.95
VOL. 97 – ROCK BAND	00700703 / $14.99
VOL. 98 – ROCK BAND	00700704 / $14.95
VOL. 99 – ZZ TOP	00700762 / $14.99
VOL. 100 – B.B. KING	00700466 / $14.99
VOL. 102 – CLASSIC PUNK	00700769 / $14.99
VOL. 103 – SWITCHFOOT	00700773 / $16.99
VOL. 104 – DUANE ALLMAN	00700846 / $16.99
VOL. 106 – WEEZER	00700958 / $14.99
VOL. 108 – THE WHO	00701053 / $14.99
VOL. 109 – STEVE MILLER	00701054 / $14.99
VOL. 111 – JOHN MELLENCAMP	00701056 / $14.99
VOL. 113 – JIM CROCE	00701058 / $14.99
VOL. 114 – BON JOVI	00701060 / $14.99
VOL. 115 – JOHNNY CASH	00701070 / $14.99
VOL. 116 – THE VENTURES	00701124 / $14.99
VOL. 119 – AC/DC CLASSICS	00701356 / $14.99
VOL. 120 – PROGRESSIVE ROCK	00701457 / $14.99
VOL. 123 – LENNON & MCCARTNEY ACOUSTIC	00701614 / $16.99

Complete song lists available online.

Prices, contents, and availability subject to change without notice.

FOR MORE INFORMATION, SEE YOUR LOCAL MUSIC DEALER, OR WRITE TO:

HAL•LEONARD® CORPORATION
7777 W. BLUEMOUND RD. P.O. BOX 13819 MILWAUKEE, WI 53213

Visit Hal Leonard online at www.halleonard.com